WHERE ARE YOU, GOD?

Michelle McKinney Hammond

DI1016875

HARVEST HOUSE PUBLISHERS
Eugene, Oregon 97402

Unless otherwise indicated, all Scripture quotations are taken from the Holy Bible: New International Version®. NIV®. Copyright © 1973, 1978, 1984 by the International Bible Society. Used by permission of Zondervan Publishing House. The "NIV" and "New International Version" trademarks are registered in the United States Patent and Trademark Office by International Bible Society.

Verses marked NLT are taken from the *Holy Bible,* New Living Translation, copyright ©1996. Used by permission of Tyndale House Publishers, Inc., Wheaton, Illinois 60189, U.S.A. All rights reserved.

Verses marked KJV are taken from the King James Version of the Bible.

Cover by Koechel Peterson & Associates, Minneapolis, Minnesota

WHERE ARE YOU, GOD?
(Formerly *His Love Always Finds Me*)
Copyright © 1999 by Michelle McKinney Hammond
Published by Harvest House Publishers
Eugene, Oregon 97402

Library of Congress Cataloging-in-Publication Data
  McKinney Hammond, Michelle, 1957–
    [His love always finds me]
    Where are you, God? / Michelle McKinney Hammond.
        p. cm.
    ISBN 0-7369-0951-6
    1. Bible—Biography—Meditations.   2. Solitude—Religious aspects—Christianity—Meditations.   I. Title.
  BS571.M373 2002
  242—dc21   2001051577

Printed in the United States of America

        02   03   04   05   06   07   / BP-CF /   10   9   8   7   6   5   4   3   2   1

In loving memory of my grandmother
Sarah Ayodele Sam.
She walked with God and was not,
for God took her,
but not before she showed me Jesus.

This one is for You, Lord.
Your love has sought me,
found me, bought me, and
kept me in Your light.
You are forever my Father,
always my Friend,
eternally the Lover of my soul.

Contents

In the Heart of the Inner Journey

WHERE ARE
YOU,
GOD?

*I*n the alone place
fear closes in as I sense my aloneness
the part of me without You
that is lost
wandering in its own apprehensions
causing my spirit
to imitate a mime
pressing against invisible walls
that soundlessly threaten
suffocation by unconscious
yet deliberate isolation
And I long for the resuscitation
that Your breath brings
giving life to all my members
strength to my soul
causing me to unfold
like a wet new butterfly
fighting to unwrap itself
from the bondage of its
self-imposed cocoon
to spread new and unfamiliar members
for the very first time
testing their strength
readying these fragile members
for the act of ascending
not caring for the fact
that it is the struggle
which produces strength
to take wing and fly
while resisting the urge
to cast off my independence
and call upon Your help
I weary myself
and wonder at my ability
to continue on
to rise above
where I presently lie…

This place is not kind
to my spirit's expectations
and I am lost in the prison of myself
while You patiently hold the key and wait...
wait for me to invite You into this alone place...
But I have learned of
another space called time
that calls sweetly to me
that woos me gently to its bosom
causing me to rest in the discovery
that it is in the alone times
that I find You
refreshing me like newly falling dew
washing me in my own tears
imparting Your comfort
like liquid oil soothing my heart
melting my defenses
and all the reasons
why I deny You
until I find myself back in this place
where fellowship is sweet communion
where intimacy is second nature
where I am reminded of Your faithfulness
and Your love for me...
yet there is a time called alone that I fear
but cannot seem to flee
for an invisible arm grips me suddenly
unexpectedly
while supports I counted true vanish
daring me to keep
my standards
in the face of a million opposing voices
I stand in the cold
shivering from my own indecision
torn by the reality
of how little I trust You
as my stomach knots in hunger
for one word of reassurance
from You who holds the key to my wholeness
that I am really not alone...

Still there is a place called alone that I seek
tucked beneath the arm of God
warm and sweet
a place where I can lay my weariness
and unanswerable questions
finding revelation in the rest
that His heartbeat gives
as I burrow
deeper into the fold of His breast
lost in the depths of His mysteries
and riches untold
found in His love
that always finds me
when I feel most alone
It is here that I find that the alone place
is no more than my own personal winter
where all that is in me dies
A season of the soul
pressed between the tendency
of my flesh
and my heart to measure time
give it walls that hem in my spirit
and torment my faith
And so I wait for spring
and the warmth of the Son
to release me
from the coldness of fear
I throw my arms open surrendering to the light
until I find myself
basking in Your love
reveling
in the alone times...

In Solitude

And when they
were alone, he expounded
all things to his disciples.

MARK 4:34 KJV

I go to the garden alone
while the dew is still on the roses,
and the sound I hear falling on my ear
the Son of God discloses…
And He walks with me
and He talks with me
and He tells me I am His own
and the joy we share as we tarry there
none other has ever known….

Sweet Times

And the Lord God took the man,
and put him into the Garden of Eden
to dress it and to keep it.

GENESIS 2:15 KJV

Adam experienced something that no other man or woman (not even Eve) on the face of the earth has ever experienced. He had the incredible privilege of having God all to himself. In the beginning it was just him and God. Though Jesus and the Holy Ghost were present, the mystery of their Oneness was very evident. Every evening they had a date, and Adam had God's full attention. No interruptions in the prayer line. No one with a more urgent request. Just Adam and God.

Can you imagine such a sublime existence? To rise each morning and watch the sun stretch its arms across the sky in praise to God on High...to watch the flowers awaken, tilting their faces in serene worship toward their Creator while the rivers that run through the garden play a symphony of exuberant celebration against the banks of the shore and the birds sing their accompaniment, welcoming the morning and thanking God for another glorious day....No telephone ringing, no alarm going off, just the gentle breeze ever so gently rousing you, stirring your lashes, tickling your nose, almost kissing you, beckoning you to arise....This was Adam's world. He rose to walk on a dew-covered carpet of grass, its pungent freshness filling the air with each step. Joyfully going about his tasks, anticipating his favorite time of the day....

And just about the time Adam thought he would burst with expectation, it happened. The atmosphere in the garden changed. The animals stood still, ears tuned to something that no one saw. The birds stopped singing, waiting for a sound that was sweeter than their own. Even the wind seemed to hold its breath. And the sun came down for a closer look, leaving golden streaks across the sky to mark its place. Then the air was filled with the incense of the Lord's presence! The Lord God Himself had descended to the garden to walk and talk, face to face, with Adam. Nothing stood between them, for Adam was naked and unashamed. Perfect and good in every way. An extension of his Abba Father. A mirror reflection of the Trinity, a living, breathing soul, unstained by sin.

It was...indescribable glory, this time of sweet communing. Every living thing in the garden seemed to be in a suspended state of reverent awe, clinging to God's every Word. His still, small voice was like music. It was like the sound of falling rain, the sound of many waters, the ebbing of the tide. It rose and fell as He shared all that He was with Adam. God's words ignited Adam's soul and brought waves of refreshment to his spirit while Adam's worship of Him brought pleasure to His heart. It was a time of intimate fellowship...of deep communion...of unspeakable expressions and wordless impartations between man and his God. And then God withdrew with the promise of returning, His presence still lingering in the air like heady perfume.

When was the last time you spent quality time alone with God? If we could only find our way back to the garden…This is the place in the cool of the evening of our lives when we finally grow still, finding our way back home. Back into the presence of God. Able once again to be open, vulnerable, honest, and uninhibited in the arms of the One who loves us most. To shut out the sound of every other voice and just listen, drinking in His Spirit. It is here that the world and all of its pressures and struggles become mere shadows that fade away as His comfort surrounds us. This is where we find peace, where we find refreshment. More importantly, this is where we find the center of our own being. This is where we find the strength to begin again.

Heavenly Father, help me to find my way back to our place of intimacy. It seems I don't visit this place enough. And yet when I finally meet You here, I wonder why it took me so long. Holy Spirit, call me and draw me to this place until my flesh rejoices to yield and enter into this sweet sanctuary of fellowship with You that my soul treasures. O Lord, help me to be as consistent in seeking You as You are in seeking me. Help me to keep ever fresh in my mind the joy of our last meeting, and never to lose the longing for more of You. In Jesus' name, amen.

Communing Times

And Enoch walked with God;
and he was not;
for God took him.

Genesis 5:24 KJV

"He's out again, is he?" the visitor asked. Enoch's wife nodded her head in reply as she stirred the evening meal over the fire. "Where is it exactly that he goes?" questioned his friend, brows drawn together in perplexed punctuation. This was the third time he had tried to visit Enoch this week, only to find that he was nowhere to be found. "Wherever their conversation takes him," Enoch's wife serenely answered. She had grown used to these times. They did not frighten or disturb her. She only had to look into Enoch's eyes when he returned to know where he had been. Sometimes he was gone for an hour. Sometimes for days. And when he returned, his body weary but his eyes gleaming with a brilliant fire that burned from within, she knew he had been with God.

What they discussed she could only imagine. She herself tried to understand how it was possible for man and

God to commune on such an intimate level. She tried to worship Him in the best way she knew, but she really couldn't say that God had ever spoken back. Enoch said it was because she didn't truly listen. She tried to listen, yet she heard nothing. She had grown beyond being jealous of her husband's deep, personal exchanges with God, choosing instead to let him share with her parts of their conversations. And, oh! What incredible things they were! Stories of what was to come. At first Enoch would eagerly tell these things to anyone who would listen. But many of these revelations were too deep, too awesome to be understood by those simply trying to keep up with their daily agenda of eking out a living for themselves. So more and more Enoch withdrew to his walks with God. He still returned with that same intense light burning in his eyes, but these days he also seemed increasingly pensive, as if his spirit were deeply pondering something profound and unspeakable. This she could respect.

Amazingly, no one ridiculed Enoch. Rather, they respectfully conceded that he truly was a man who sought God diligently. All who knew him admired this, and even promised themselves that they, too, would draw closer to God as soon as they got a little extra time on their hands. It was obvious that Enoch pleased God; he was blessed above and beyond measure. No one in their right mind would ever guess that he was three hundred and sixty-five years old. Why, he didn't look a day over one hundred and he was still having children! It was as if Enoch's conversations with God renewed his strength like the eagles'. He was always so full of energy. But what could they possibly find to talk about for hours—sometimes days—on end? Though many speculated, no one volunteered to accompany Enoch as he set off to fellowship with the Lord. It would have been almost impolite to do so, a most unwelcome intrusion. Yet countless eyes followed Enoch as he walked to his place of solitude to be with…Him….

And so his wife prepared dinner and waited for his return. Once again she meditated upon how different her husband seemed these days after his time alone with God. More contemplative, lost in all he had been told. In the past he would return more vocal, warning his neighbors of God's judgment against those who were godless. But these days Enoch was silent, as if waiting for something to happen.

Slowly the night settled down around her. The embers of the dinner fire had died, and still she waited for his return. The air around her held a tension she did not recognize, and she wondered what was different about this night. Then a voice, or perhaps it was just a quiet understanding, rose from within her spirit. "He won't be back," it whispered softly. She contemplated these words, quietly releasing her beloved husband into the hands of his Lord as she fell into a peaceful sleep.

And now here was his friend again, inquiring when Enoch would return. Why couldn't he understand what she so clearly knew? Enoch would not be back, for God had taken him. Yet this friend still insisted on searching for him. And everyone wondered at her serenity in the face of such deeply disturbing circumstances. "Poor dear," they all thought as they saw her set out, beginning the familiar pattern of her late husband. "Perhaps she will find him in one of her walks." Little did they know it was not Enoch she was seeking.

Enoch, the seventh generation born from Adam, was the foreshadow of yet another man who would literally be translated into the heavenly realm while still wrapped in living mortal flesh. Enoch had an extraordinary relationship with God, a deep intimacy, and a reputation that brought pleasure to the heart of the Father. For this he was rewarded by escaping the sting of death. Though this is the type of relationship with God we have the best of intentions to achieve, so many things distract us away from pressing into that place with Him.

How many times do we promise to spend more time communing with our Father? How many times do we come into His presence so laden down with our own cares that we hurriedly dump them at His feet, then dash away to extinguish yet another fire in our lives? And then we hear someone repeat something that God told them and we listen in envy, wondering, Why doesn't God tell me things like that? Why doesn't He tell me anything, period? With chagrin, we realize that we've been far too busy talking at God to listen to Him. And yet the only way to be translated to a place far above our circumstances is to immerse ourselves in Him.

> *Dear Heavenly Father, please forgive me for my misplaced priorities. Forgive me for answering the call of the world instead of stealing away with You. Although I know I was created for Your good pleasure, I spend far too much time seeking pleasures of my own. As You await me becoming a true worshiper who will worship You in spirit and in truth, I fill my world with helpless idols and seek more blatant answers that won't require any surrender or transparency on my part. And though I long to please You, I fear what I will become if I do all that You require. Help me to forsake all but Your heart and find my pleasure in pleasing You. Help me to realize that my greatest reward at the end of the day is You and the power You possess to translate me above all that binds me. In Jesus' name, amen.*

Binding Times

When the sun went down, and it was dark, behold a smoking furnace, and a burning lamp that passed between those pieces. In the same day the LORD made a covenant with Abram.

GENESIS 15:17,18 KJV

Abram didn't know if it was the night air or beholding this sight, both awesome and terrible, that caused him to be chilled to the bone. He felt every hair on his body stand on end as the presence of God saturated his understanding with visions of things that God would not speak. However, His demonstration spoke loud and clear. Abram had pondered the Lord's words all afternoon as he gathered together a heifer, a goat, a ram, a dove, and a young pigeon. "I will be your great reward..." The words echoed in his spirit as he cut each animal in two, with the exception of the birds, and arranged the halves opposite each other in obedience to God. "I will be your great reward..." *What could that possibly mean?* thought Abram. *How could God being my reward solve my immediate problems?*

He felt an ache every time he saw the look on his wife's face as she gazed at a mother holding her child. And he felt helpless. Helpless to give Sarai the one thing she truly wanted—a son. Truly, God had richly blessed them with everything else. But this one thing. This one thing was like a wet blanket snuffing out the joy of everything else. How could God being his reward resolve this conflict between joy and pain, comfort and longing? Yet Abram willingly obeyed his Lord, preparing the animals He requested, and he waited. For the Lord had promised him descendants as numerous as the stars, and Abram believed Him. God had called him out and away from all that he was accustomed to with the promise of possessing a new land, and He had proven Himself along the way, increasing Abram's wealth in measures untold. Yet this one thing was different from any other area of his life. His other prayers had been answered almost instantly, but this one thing lingered. It became a greater question day by day. As time became a foe against his desire, his need for a greater assurance from God became increasingly pressing.

And now God had given him a sign. An awesome sign, sealing his promise to Abram that his descendants, birthed from his own seed, would be more numerous than the stars. More numerous than his ability to count. And greater still, his descendants would possess this new land that God had brought him to! This was more than he had dared hope for, yet he believed God's promise. But still this nagging need for affirmation burned within his heart. And now here in this place of meeting, as the sun sought solace from the heat of the day on the backside of the hills, Abram fought the exhaustion of his efforts to wait on God. To hear a clear word. To receive some sign, some indication that God would keep this promise he was almost afraid to cling to. Then God's whisper interrupted the dusk, answering Abram's questions with dreadful revelations as He unfolded the fate of Abram's lineage yet to come. The darkness of separation that his people would feel as they experienced the bonds of slavery in Egypt before returning to this land. Abram could not imagine this. As long as he had known God, he had known liberty and wealth.

Abram recalled the day he first heard God's voice telling him to forsake everything he held dear and follow Him away from his family and his country to a new land that He would show him. Something told him he could trust this voice, and he followed willingly. Still, their relationship had never been tested in this way. Feeling the need for more visible support, he took his nephew Lot with him. Abram soon found out why the Lord had suggested that he go alone. God had known all along that those outside of the vision He gives become a time-consuming distraction from the true blessing that awaits. In time, Abram learned he had no need for Lot or to cling to familiar crutches, so the two men parted company. Abram came to trust God as a constant in his life; truly, He was "the friend that sticketh closer than a brother" (Proverbs 18:24 KJV).

So here Abram was—where God had wanted him to be in the first place—alone with Him. In His presence nothing overshadowed Him, not even the sun. And so in the darkness of its absence, God became Abram's only light. As the blood flowed between the carcasses, it was joined by a smoking firepot and a flaming torch, sealing the matter between this man and his God. Yes, God would keep His Word. Even this one thing was not too difficult for Him to accomplish. With this knowledge, God sealed His promise to Abram by literally putting His Word on the line, making a binding covenant through the fire, the light, and the blood. And because He had no one greater to swear by, He swore by Himself to bring to pass what He had promised in His own irrevocable way.

What is the desire that you feel isolated in harboring? It's important to remember that when our desires surround our heart so tightly that we feel alone inside of our dreams, God is present lighting the way, holding a flaming torch aloft to guide our steps toward our destiny, making us worthy to receive the promise with the purifying fire of His own holiness and the cleansing flow of sacrificial blood.

> *Heavenly Father, You have blessed me in so many*
> *ways that I almost feel ashamed to ask You for one*
> *more thing. And yet my heart is overwhelmed with*
> *longing and my desire weighs heavily upon my soul. I*
> *feel as if You've said yes, but the promise seems to*
> *take so long to become a manifested reality. I*
> *wonder if Your promise is simply my imagination*
> *and my own flesh willing You to be in agreement*
> *with me. As I lay my longing at Your feet once more,*
> *please speak a sure word to my spirit. Grant me Your*
> *assurance that You will come bearing the answer*
> *and lighting the way to my heart's treasure. In Jesus'*
> *name, amen.*

Pensive Times

Now Isaac had come from Beer Lahai Roi, for he was
living in the Negev. He went out to the field one evening
to meditate, and as he looked up, he saw camels approaching.

GENESIS 24:62,63

saac closed his eyes and took a deep breath. There was something special about the evening air. It was...more moist, more fragrant, as if it were releasing a million secrets that had been tucked away from the stare of the noonday sun. Too fragile. Too precious to risk being scorched by such brilliant attention, the secrets waited for a safer time of day to make their presence known. Isaac took another deep breath and let the breeze soothe his thoughts. He missed his mother dearly. The thought of her brought both delight and sadness. Delight at the memories, sadness at her death.

As Isaac had been born to Abraham and Sarah in their late years, he had been their joy. No child could be more affirmed than he was as he reveled in a close relationship with both his father and mother. His father taught him of

God, his mother taught him of unconditional love—a love she poured out with fervor as if attempting to make up for lost time, whether from past or future, he could not tell. But a willing recipient Isaac was, enjoying all the attention. And then the day he never prepared himself for came. As subtle as the shades of gray that sneak between the yellow lines of sunlight when dusk takes its position in the sky, a final sleep came upon Sarah and she was gone. With her exit came the most excruciating grief. And now his only solace were these stolen moments of meditation. These times of silent exchange with God. These times of waiting for the burdens of the heart to be lifted. Waiting for some rhyme or reason to be given to his days. He, like his father, waited to hear what God had to say.

Tonight, Isaac noticed a slight lift from the heaviness he had been feeling. A sense of new hope mingled ever so slightly with a touch of apprehension. His father had sent their servant Eliezer to find him a wife. A wife! The thought excited and frightened him at the same time. What could he allow himself to expect? Would she be as beautiful as his mother Sarah had been? Would she be kind and sweet and loving? Would she be an understanding friend and loving companion? His father had been very adamant about him marrying from among their own people, and that was fine with Isaac. Still, it was a little unnerving to wait for this someone to be unveiled. After all, he was the one who would have to live with this woman all the days of his life! Although it would not have been traditional for him to choose his own wife, a part of him wondered if he would feel better if he could. Not knowing seemed to make the waiting even more unbearable, realizing that the choice was completely out of his hands. Isaac was at the mercy of God, left to count the moments of interminable suspense. No one could make him feel better...no one but God.

This was the fragile part of trusting God that his father Abraham had seemed to master, while Isaac himself was not sure he would ever fully arrive at this lofty summit of faith. He believed that God knew what was best for him, but he wondered if God really cared or considered what he liked as well. And so he prayed, "Oh, God, allow her to be all that You know I need as well as everything that would bring pleasure to my heart." Could it be that God said yes? Was His reply in the breeze that swept across Isaac's shoulders as if to give him a reassuring squeeze? He turned to see if he could catch a glimpse of God as his father had one great and unforgettable evening, and then he saw her....He felt rooted to the spot, but only for a moment. His heart was pounding in his ears as he started toward the familiar camels of his father's house that were approaching in the distance. As he watched Eliezer help his bride down from her camel, he breathed one last "Please…" under his breath to God and went to greet her. But he knew even before he reached her that she was the answer to all his prayers. He knew from the tilt of her head. The poetry of her movement. The sound of her voice. He knew that God had sent him a comforter, a friend, and a lover. He took her into his mother's tent, where she became his wife and he loved her. And in her arms the pain of loss and change were transformed into deep rivers of joy and healing.

We tend to feel that what God has in mind for us is kind of like oatmeal— good for us, but not exactly what we consider a fun dish.

What things have you found yourself clinging to that need to be released to God? It's natural to be a little hesitant to let go and allow God to make the crucial choices in our lives. We sometimes feel isolated and helpless when we are not actively involved in manipulating the details that make up the big picture of our desires. Somehow we find ourselves becoming distrustful of God and His agenda for our lives. We tend to feel that what God has in mind for us is kind of like oatmeal—good for us, but not exactly what we consider a fun dish. "If I allow Him to choose my mate, my career, my purpose in life, who knows what I'll get? Or where I'll end up?" we think in panic. And then God presents us with gifts that cause us to be ashamed we ever thought such things when we unwrap gifts our eyes have never seen, our ears never heard, and our hearts never imagined. He surprises us with joy every time, and in these moments we rejoice at our lack of control. We revel in the opportunity to showcase yet another trophy of God's incredible ability to bless us above and beyond our finite human comprehension of what it takes to bring us overwhelming fulfillment.

> *Dear Heavenly Father, please forgive me for all the times I placed my desires upon Your altar only to snatch them back in fear that You would not fill them in the way my heart required. Please help me to unwrap my fingers from grasping too tightly the idea of how I think things ought to be in my life. Help me to completely release myself, my desires, and all concerning my life into Your care, knowing that You care for me. That it is Your desire to shower me with good and perfect gifts. Perfect from where You sit, and perfect for where I live. Help me to find my peace in trusting You implicitly and rejoicing in the choices You make concerning me, keeping in mind that all these things are working for the good to the ultimate end of producing fruit and reproducing joy in my life now and Your kingdom ever more. In Jesus' name, amen.*

Awesome Times

When Jacob awoke from his sleep, he thought, "Surely the LORD is in this place, and I was not aware of it." He was afraid and said, "How awesome is this place! This is none other than the house of God; this is the gate of heaven."

GENESIS 28:16,17

$\mathcal{S}$till wiping the sleep from his eyes, Jacob tried to separate reality from his dreams but found the two immutably bound. There was no separating them. The stairway from heaven to earth was real. The angels ascending and descending were no hazy vision. The angel of the Lord was no apparition, for his promise rang true. He had indeed been visited by God in this place. There was no one to deny or confirm what was happening here, just his own soul bearing witness to this incredible happening. But what his comprehension could not grasp was why? Why would God promise him anything? Especially after what he had done. Didn't God know what everybody else knew—that Jacob was here in the wilderness because of his own underhandedness? Why did this God, who insisted on holiness according to his father, feel he was worthy to receive such a promise?

The blessing he had deceitfully taken from his father's hands and stolen from his brother's legacy God now freely gave without any tricks on his part. Jacob didn't know how to respond. He was used to tit for tat. Some sort of bargain had to be struck. After all, no one ever got anything for free. So Jacob decided to forge his own deal with God, on his own terms, in order to solidify their understanding. If God would be with him, provide for him, and bring him back to this place, *then* he, Jacob, would give God permission to be his God. And God silently agreed, watched Jacob go his own way, and waited for him to discover that the only One who truly kept His promises was God Himself. But they were ultimately made on His terms.

So Jacob bargained with Laban for the hand of Rachel and found himself betrayed. The trickster had finally met his match. Only the mercy of God could give him the upper hand. God gracefully kept His promise, preserving him even in the face of Laban's cleverness until it was clearly apparent to Jacob what must become obvious to us all—that "but for the grace of God go I." Yet God had more to teach him.

After years of struggling to live one step ahead of his father-in-law's manipulations, Jacob finally headed home. Surrounded by all of his possessions, his household, his children, and his wives, he felt rather fortified until he received news that his brother Esau was on his way to meet him. With this news, the old Jacob returned. Trusting the Lord was out, and leaning to his own understanding was in big time.

After sending his entourage and family ahead, Jacob found himself alone in the very place he had been avoiding. Forsaken by his own wiles and schemes, he was now forced to depend totally on God at the most threatening point in his life. This was a completely new experience for Jacob, and he wrestled with it. *How do I get rid of myself?* he wondered. *How do I get to the place of "No longer I, but God in me," when "me" is all I've relied on for as long as I can remember?* Jacob was frightened. He was letting go to release himself into God-only-knows what instead of holding on to *something*, even if it was "puttin' a hurtin'" on him, as the old folks say. And so the angel of the Lord allowed Jacob to wrestle with him until the break of day. To the breaking point. For it is only at the breaking point that we begin to see the light.

And still Jacob clung, afraid to let go without an assurance, a blessing, from God. Jacob was still clinging to what Jacob knew. But no blessing came until Jacob admitted who he was—which was *where* he was. And then the grace of God released him to be a new man. A man outside of himself. Whole and free. Naked and wounded by the knowledge that he had gained nothing in his own strength but that which God had allowed. How much easier life would have been if Jacob had simply yielded to the hand of the One who freely gives! But the greater tragedy would have been if he'd never arrived at this point of understanding.

What things in your life have you felt the necessity to take care of yourself? In this "you've got to make it happen" world, we've gotten snowed into thinking we have to "help God" in order to obtain what we think we want or need. And we, like Jacob, often find ourselves forsaken by our own machinations. Suffering from the backlash of what we considered a successful manipulation, we attempt to strike another bargain, then find ourselves in even deeper trouble.

Flailing, wrestling, unwilling to let go of the old way of doing things, we hang on for dear life, determined to make it work. And God quietly says, "Let go," to which we reply, "No! Not until You show me what I'm going to get out of this!" He fails to answer, but instead poses another question: "Who do you think you are?" But the real question is, "Who are you, really? And how much further do you think you can get without My assistance?" And we are forced to grudgingly admit our finiteness and deposit our limping egos into the arms of God, who blesses us in spite of ourselves.

> *Dear Heavenly Father, I admit my own weakness. I admit my own attempts to assist You in blessing me have failed miserably. I even admit that my own self-ishness has caused me to grasp at my own desires with no thought of those around me. So I deposit all that I've gained for myself back at Your feet. All of my fleshly manipulations, plots, and schemes. I lay them beside my dreams and offer them back to You. I know that in Your fairness, You will bless me without costing others. Please forgive me for my lack of trusting Your heart toward me. Help me to rest more securely in Your love and Your desire to bless me above measure. Help me not to be moved by what my eyes see, but only what my heart hears from You. In Jesus' name, amen.*

There You are!
I thought I had lost You
but instead I have found You
where You've always been
Still my Father
Still my Friend
Still my source of Consolation
Soothing all the places
that were ravaged from
strangers who caught me
wandering down my own path
seeking my own way
which always leads me
back to You
back to who I truly am....

Revealing Times

Now Moses was tending the flock of Jethro his father-in-law,
the priest of Midian, and he led the flock to the far side
of the desert and came to Horeb, the mountain of God.
There the angel of the LORD appeared to him
in flames of fire from within a bush.

EXODUS 3:1,2

Moses stooped to remove his sandals with trembling fingers, wondering to himself at the strange sight he beheld. Not knowing whether to hide his face or to sneak another look, he cowered in awe at this apparition...*or was it?* He couldn't tell. But then again, this... phenomenon (yes, that was a better word for it) had a voice. This vision claimed to be God and, more incredibly, said He wanted to use him, Moses, to deliver the Israelites out of the bondage they suffered in Egypt! Didn't He know that Moses was a man on the run? Didn't He know of his crime? Didn't He know he couldn't talk properly? If He were truly God, then surely He would know that Moses was hardly qualified for such a lofty mission!

Yes, he had been raised in Pharaoh's house. Yes, he knew the ins and outs of the court. Yes, he had been

trained in all manner of Egyptian knowledge and eti-
quette. BUT…and this was a very big but…everyone
knew by now that Moses was a Hebrew with no power
himself, reduced to living as a fugitive. It seemed that he
was always out of place, a fish out of water, isolated from
those around him because he was different. From the day
his mother placed him in a handwoven basket and sailed
him down the Nile in order to save his life he became a
stranger among the familiar. Rescued and raised by the
Pharaoh's daughter, the tug to be grateful and enjoy an
enviable fate was juxtaposed with championing the cause
of his people who did not share as posh a life as he. He
was caught between two cultures, considered an outsider
to both. To the Egyptians he was a Hebrew, a mere charity
case they indulged for the sake of Pharaoh's daughter who
sheltered him under her care. To the Hebrews he was a
wannabe who had denied his roots to live in Pharaoh's
house. Even the relationship between his brother Aaron,
his sister Miriam, and himself, though loving, seemed
strained. And who could blame them? They lived worlds
apart even though in close proximity, their experiences
totally foreign to one another.

    And now after killing a cruel Egyptian overseer, he had
fled to Midian to escape the wrath of Pharaoh. What could
God be thinking? How could He send him back to Egypt?
What welcome would he find there after all this time? Who
could he truly call family? What lineage could he point to
in order to validate himself in the eyes of those he was
called to lead? Who would be on his side? Yet God said He
would be with him. But who was this God? What were His
credentials? Who would Moses say had sent him? And then
came the words that made Moses' heart explode…
"I Am That I Am." "I Am That I Am…" "I Am That I Am!"
Within those words were a million answers! I Am He who
gives sight to the blind, speech to the mute, strength to the

weak, faith to the helpless, provision to those who lack, security to the wandering, a deliverer to the bound... whatever it is that you need, I Am that! And right now Moses needed a lot. He needed courage. He needed affirmation. Affirmation that he belonged. Belonged to someone, that his roots were secure, that there was someone in his life who truly had his back. And here was God saying He was all that Moses was searching for.

But just in case that wasn't enough for Moses, He would allow his brother Aaron to assist him in this important assignment although this was not His preference. And so, with the assistance of Aaron's eloquent speech and God's miracles to back him up, Moses found security in his calling and led the people of Israel out. But even this great success was not enough to make his heart at home among his people. He still felt the gulf between them. They were hesitant to approach God for themselves, yet were antagonistic toward what they termed his position of favor with God. After all, who was he to tell them what to do? Just because he got to see God face to face, why should he lord it over them? Poor Moses couldn't win for losing. The more he tried to accommodate their insecurities in order to be accepted, the more they misinterpreted his benevolence for spiritual pride. In the end when God's wrath burned against the people, the same ones he defended cost him his dream—to enter the Promise Land. Yes, Moses learned the hard way that in the face of "Who do you think you are?" there can only be one answer: Because He Is, I am. No apologies.

In Him our identity is made secure.
The search ends before His throne.

Who am I?" many of us ask. In search of our identity it is important to know that it really doesn't matter who we are as long as He Is. In Him our identity is made secure. The search ends before His throne. Once yielded to His Spirit He illuminates our understanding and unfolds the mystery of who we really are and who He has created us to be. This is privileged information for us and us alone. If no one else gets it, that's all right because it doesn't change God's design. So let them murmur and know when to let go of the stragglers, releasing yourself back into the arms of the One who knows you best.

Dear Heavenly Father, I am so guilty of trying to win everyone's approval except Yours and it always costs me a piece of myself. Why the search for outward validation consumes me I will never know, but You do. You see to the core of my soul. I ask that You would make me secure in You. That the search for who I really am would end before Your presence. Fill me with Yourself and who You are. Let me rejoice in my new identity as You write Your name upon my heart. You are my Abba Father and in that I can rest. And when I've come to the end of myself and I question my own identity lead me back to the truth that in You I am. In Jesus' name, amen.

Because You are
I Am
all that I hope for
all that I dream of
even that which
I am afraid to see
for all that
I am
is hidden in You
revealed in Your light
and manifested
in my surrender to You.
You are
I Am....

Challenging Times

*When the angel of the LORD appeared to Gideon, he said,
"The LORD is with you, mighty warrior."
"But sir," Gideon replied, "if the Lord is with us,
why has all this happened to us?..."*

JUDGES 6:13

Glancing furtively over his shoulder to make sure no one was watching, Gideon tossed the wheat into the air and watched the kernels lift and separate from the chaff as the wind interrupted their upward ascent. He thought back to the days when he enjoyed the kiss of the sun on his shoulders and the exhilaration of the breeze sweeping across his face as he threshed his harvest atop a hill. It was such a liberating feeling to be out in the open air, watching the wheat sparkle as it twirled upward. It was amazing how it took no more than a gust of wind to divide the empty from that which was essential. Gideon pondered this often as he repeated the process year after year. But now those times of enjoyment were over. They had been over for seven years. He had been reduced to doing this task secretly in a winepress, away from the eyes of those who were his people's enemies—the Midianites.

For far too long the countryside had groaned under the terrorism and destruction of this band of nomads who timed their visitations with the harvest. For seven years the Israelites planted their crops. And for seven years the Midianites, Amalekites and other eastern peoples invaded the country, destroying all that they planted and killing all their herds until they were reduced to being fugitives in their own land—preparing shelters for themselves in mountain clefts, caves, and strongholds; trying to salvage what they could under cover; wondering aloud if God would ever deliver them.

And now sensing an unknown presence in his private sanctuary, Gideon, fearing discovery by an enemy, whirled around to face a stranger who seemed to appear out of nowhere and greet him with even stranger words. Him, a warrior? He in no way felt like a warrior. Try victim. Try defeated. But hardly would a warrior be found skulking around in this manner, barely eking out an existence. And if God was with him, He sure had a funny way of showing it. As for being the chosen vessel to save his people out of the hand of the Midianites, that was truly a laugh! He was the least in his family, his clan was the weakest in Manasseh, was this some sort of cruel joke? Yet something inside of him dared to hope, dared to make a sacrifice, dared to listen to what this bearer of these unbelievable tidings had to say.

As the offering was consumed, Gideon's faith was ignited. A boldness that was willing to shatter the altars of compromise his people had built rose up within him. Yet not inclined to face the wrath of his family and the men of the town, he chose the shelter of night along with ten of his servants to annihilate his father's altar to Baal and the Asherah pole beside it. His spirit felt the same exhilaration he felt on the hilltops while threshing as he burnt a sacrifice to the Lord with the wood that had once been a memorial to a foreign god. Truly, the wheat was now being separated from the chaff.

Just as Gideon suspected would be the case, the town's cries of indignation rose with the morning sun in a loud, discordant chorus. Perhaps his father Joash, surveying the remains of the sacrifice, was jolted into remembering the former days when the Lord God had shown Himself mighty on their behalf. For now he steadfastly defended his son, declaring that if Baal were truly the god they thought he was, then he should rise to his own defense. Feeling totally affirmed by his father and girded up by the Spirit of the Lord coming upon him, Gideon sounded the trumpet to arms against their enemies, no longer feeling alone. And God, not willing to share His glory with a large company of men, did a final threshing and separating before allowing Gideon and his elite army to proceed onward to victory. God showed Himself to be ever present in Gideon's life, and Gideon became a mighty man of valor, no longer fearful of stepping out against those who challenged him.

How often do we wonder where God is in the midst of situations that repeatedly beat us down time and time again? Our faith often becomes lost in the shuffle of dire circumstances that life continually deals us. We stumble into compromising our standards in order to survive, tripping over the enemy's lies that we are insignificant, disowned, unloved, and defenseless. But then the Lord Himself goes before us and clears the way, reminding us that if we don't walk in total trust and obedience before Him, victory will remain elusive.

> *Dear Heavenly Father, forgive me for the many times I walked away from You devising my own way, then turned back again to question Your lack of faithfulness. Forgive me for the idols I have built that block my vision of You standing there waiting to assist me out of my troubles. Please help me to tear down the idols in my life and call on You and You alone. Help me to resist the urge to compromise my standards because of my lack of trust in You. Help me to internalize Your promises and stand on them with unwavering allegiance. Help me to separate the lies of the enemy from Your truth. Liberate me to rest in Your strength, knowing that You are my defense and my deliverer. In Jesus' name, amen.*

Broken Times

*He awoke from his sleep and thought, "I'll go out
as before and shake myself free." But he did not
know that the LORD had left him.*

JUDGES 16:20

Samson squirmed to find a more comfortable position on the dank floor of the prison. The bronze shackles that bound his ankles chafed against his skin and left their mildewed marks like green tattoos. He smoothed the fresh new locks of hair back from his forehead, thinking how ironic it was that the thing that had gotten him into the most trouble was gone too late—his eyes. His eyes had always gotten him in trouble. For instance, he wished he had never laid eyes on Delilah. And now what he could no longer see haunted him night after night in dreams that turned quickly to nightmares filled with a million screaming regrets. How could he have been such a fool? Philistine women couldn't be trusted. Why hadn't he learned his lesson with the Philistine girl he had married? His parents had tried to tell him, but no, he wouldn't listen. After all, he was invincible. Who could hurt him? Samson learned too late that he was his most injurious enemy.

Delilah had been so beautiful, so compliant to all his fleshly wishes. She wasn't like the women from among his people, always frowning and reminding him of his calling when he wanted to indulge in a little sport. Delilah didn't care that he was a Nazirite priest; she just wanted to please him. And he just wanted to be pleased. After all, being a judge over Israel was hard work. Settling disputes, leading fights against their enemies...at the end of the day he deserved a little levity, a little harmless amusement in the form of a good woman who wasn't religious or demanding. But now all that he had loved about Delilah made Samson sick to his stomach as he saw through the whole trap.

How could he have believed that she loved him? He had been so flattered when she wondered at his extraordinary strength. He had so enjoyed showing off for her, escaping the grip of the Philistines who were constantly trying to entrap him. He had teased her, making up amusing stories about the source of his strength when she asked. But her questions had become more and more insistent. She complained that he didn't really love her at all if he chose not to confide in her. And still he never thought back to when another Philistine woman who had betrayed him, his wife, had done the same. No, Samson was too caught up in the haze of her perfume and that incredible incense she burned in the room whenever he was there. His defenses were lowered by the wine she served. Of course he loved her, he argued. Could he please just get a bit of sleep, a tender kiss, a little peace? But she hounded him and hounded him until he saw no rest in sight and finally came clean with her. And she responded by dealing him the dirty hand of betrayal. Luring him to sleep in her lap, she held him in deceitful arms while her partner in crime shaved off the seven braids that held the secret of Samson's strength.

He awoke to find himself surrounded by the Philistines but forsaken by those he had counted on—Delilah, God, his own strength…gone. Those who had previously quaked in fear before him now gouged out his eyes, mercilessly dragging him away to be treated like a common slave grinding grain in a prison. Sad to say, Samson now saw clearly what he had never seen before—his own foolishness. His utter disregard for sound counsel. His disrespect of God and His calling. The needs of the people that God had entrusted into his care. All of this had escaped his vision as he focused on his own personal pursuits.

He was almost too embarrassed to ask for God's assistance now. But for as much as he had been self-indulgent, he needed to give serving God one last-ditch effort. At this point, the only redeemable effort would be to annihilate as many of the Hebrews' enemies as he could in one fatal swoop. For this he would need God's help. Finally Samson understood that he could not do this in his own strength. With this resolved, he entered the arena where the Philistines had all gathered to pay homage to their god, Dagon. And Samson asked God to be his companion once more. The body that he refused to present as a living sacrifice, to prove what had been God's good, acceptable, and perfect will concerning his life, he now realized had been his reasonable service in exchange for all that God had given him. As the pillars of the temple began to topple beneath his touch, that which he withheld before he now gladly offered. And he surmised in his final thoughts that a moment of honor birthed through the labor of obedience was far sweeter than a life filled with meaningless seductions.

Where do you feel you have failed others, yourself, and God lately? Sometimes the mistakes we've made seem unredeemable. We find ourselves bowed over in bondage to the pain of the consequences that rebellion brings. Self-debasement and condemnation make the load more than we can bear as we cringe in the mirror of our own foolishness. But God's grace meets us even in this place. And as we own up to our sin, recognizing what we refused to see before, so blinded were we with the immediate cravings of our own desires, He sends His own strength to refresh us, renew us, and help us stand again.

> *Dear Heavenly Father, so many times I allow the lust of my eyes to override the direction of Your Spirit. Please help me keep the bigger picture in view. Help me to have a greater passion for fulfilling my God-ordained destiny than fulfilling the immediate desires of the flesh. Even when I don't know all of the details, help my trust in You to be a bridge over the chasm of the questions my heart can't answer. Please meet me in my moments of failure, forgive and restore me, and give me the opportunity to triumph again. In Jesus' name, amen.*

Commissioning Times

Then Eli realized that the LORD was calling the boy.
So Eli told Samuel, "Go and lie down, and if he calls you,
say, 'Speak, LORD, for your servant is listening.'"
So Samuel went and lay down in his place.

1 SAMUEL 3:8,9

amuel lay in the dark, listening to the night sounds around him, reflecting on his mother's last visit to him. He really enjoyed his duties in the temple and Eli was just like a father to him, yet he looked forward to his mother, Hannah, coming every year bearing gifts and loads of love and comfort. These were special times in which she always reminded him of how she had prayed diligently for him and God had answered her prayer. In gratitude she had dedicated him back to the service of the Lord. "Samuel," she told him, "never forget that you are a special gift from God. You must always bring pleasure to His heart in return for His mercy and kindness." She warned him against behaving like Eli's sons who were fueling the gossip mill with their disgraceful behavior. All were horrified at their blatant disregard for the things of

God. They didn't even try to hide how they skimmed off the best of the offerings that the people brought to the Lord. And the womanizing! Everyone knew Eli's sons were sleeping with the women who worked at the entrance to the Tent of Meeting. Eli had confronted them, but they had only scorned his rebuke and continued to anger God and man with their flagrant rebellion. Samuel had purposed he would never bring sorrow to his mother's heart as Eli's sons brought to their father's.

Samuel mulled upon all of these things as he stared into the darkness, waiting for sleep to come. He thought about the stories Eli told about how God used to speak to the people and give His prophets visions of things to come. Samuel had never experienced this, and he wondered what it would be like to actually hear the voice of God. What exactly would His voice sound like? Would it be frightening or contain some distinct quality that set it apart from human voices? He would like to experience hearing God's voice one day... Just as he was drifting off to sleep, he heard a voice calling softly from the edge of his consciousness, "Samuel...Samuel..." "Yes, here I am," he replied. *Perhaps Eli is thirsty and needs a drink* he thought, getting up and walking to Eli's room. It was difficult for the old man to find his way around at night now that his sight was growing more and more dim. But much to Samuel's confusion, his hasty appearance in Eli's room jolted his mentor out of a sound sleep. *Hmm, that's strange,* he thought as he returned to his own room. *Perhaps Eli didn't call out in his sleep... Wait! There it is again.* By the third reoccurrence, Samuel stood looking befuddled at the irritated Eli, who had been roused thrice and looked none too pleased at these constant interruptions.

But slowly something dawned on Eli. This was not simply the boy's imagination. Samuel was indeed being summoned...by the Lord! His heart leapt within him. Perhaps God was once again ready to manifest Himself as He had in days gone by! And so, with Eli's gentle instruction ringing in his ears, Samuel returned to his pallet and waited to see if the Lord would call him again. It seemed as if an eternity passed but it was just a few moments before the Lord—this time he knew—came and stood before Samuel and called to him. Once. Twice. Finally Samuel found his tongue and repeated what Eli had told him to say: "Speak, for Your servant is listening."

Along with the recognition of the Lord's voice came revelations, some of which Samuel was disinclined to repeat. And so he pondered this strange new experience until morning. Lost in thought as he automatically went through his daily ritual, he was jolted from his reverie by Eli calling him; Samuel could now recognize the difference between the two voices. Reluctantly he answered, for he knew that Eli would want to know what God had said. And Samuel was unwilling to be the bearer of bad news to one who had been so kind to him. At this moment he felt isolated by the information he hid in his bosom, fearing Eli's response to the news that God was displeased with his family and that punishment would soon visit his house. Would he accuse Samuel of being a presumptuous upstart whose ego had been inflated overnight because of God's one conversation with him? And what of Eli's sons, who treated him with veiled disdain because he was so "holy" already? What if Eli told his sons that Samuel had prophesied that God was going to judge them? What cruel retaliation would they plan for him?

But Eli yielded to even this harsh news from the Lord, and Samuel was encouraged never to hide what God had disclosed to him. And God, seeing that he could trust Samuel to repeat what He relayed, continued to reveal Himself to him through His word. Samuel's boldness never failed through appointing, then impeaching Saul, and reappointing David as king over Israel. No one stood against him, for all knew that Samuel was proven as a prophet of the Lord. Truly, friendship with God was to be trusted more than the shifting approval of men.

This is the type of fellowship we long for with God. But then He comes, bearing news that isn't exactly what we had anticipated, calling us to action, making us responsible for what we've heard. *Is that truly You, Lord?* we are tempted to ask, at times not being able to discern His voice from our own opinions. Can you recall the last thing the Lord shared with you, whether through a spoken word, His written Word, or a word of encouragement from someone in your midst? Sometimes lifting the standard of God's Word in a place where it is seemingly disregarded can be most alienating. We wonder if we should say something or keep what we know to ourselves. But God stands waiting for the use of our voices; therefore, He truly stands beside us.

> *Dear Heavenly Father, I remember times when I*
> *failed to recognize Your voice. Times when the truth*
> *of Your Word was too much for me to bear. Please*
> *help me to have the courage to receive what You say*
> *and to follow You unwaveringly. Help me not to fear*
> *the faces of people when You call me to speak a*
> *word of truth, reproof, or correction to them. Still the*
> *quaking of my heart and fill me with boldness. Fill*
> *me with a passion for the truth that refuses to com-*
> *promise in the face of opposition. Help me to*
> *remember that I represent You first and foremost,*
> *and that my obedience to You is essential to my*

wholeness and peace of mind and spirit. Keep me close to You. Let not even Your whisper be lost to my ears, oh, Lord. I long to hear all that You have to say and do Your bidding. In Jesus' name, amen.

As the deer pants for streams of water,
so my soul pants for you, O God
My soul thirsts for God, for the living God.
Where can I go and meet with God?

PSALM 42:1,2

Intimate Times

I have seen you in the sanctuary and beheld your power
and your glory. Because your love is better than life,
my lips will glorify you, I will praise you as long as I live.

PSALM 63:2-4

David's eyes scanned the expanse of the wilderness. It reflected the way his spirit felt. Dry. Empty. Parched. Longing for a drop of refreshment. A fresh wind of relief. The air was as still as his heart, hoping and praying for God to move, to speak, to do something, anything that would put a period on this portion of his life. Being back in this place brought back too many memories. Some were sweet and distant, some too fresh and painful to dwell on for any length of time. It was so ironic that he, a king, would be in his present position. A fugitive in his own domain. Running from his own son. It was easier to understand why he ran from Saul many years ago. After all, Saul had been an enemy, afraid of losing his kingdom. But his own son! This treachery David took personally. Yet it was times like this that were ideal for grounding, refocusing, reassessing where he had come from.

As David backtracked through the years in his mind, he thought of the times before his household had lurched out of control, fueled by lust and bitterness. He recalled the times before his son Amnon raped his stepsister Tamar, and their brother Absalom retaliated by having Amnon murdered. He remembered the days before his own scandalous affair with Bathsheba and his shameful hit on her husband, Uriah. Even before the times of dancing victoriously before the Lord after a hard-won battle there had been simpler times. Priceless times tucked away within a secret place inside him, times spent in green pastures. Times when the Lord and his father's flocks were his only companions. This was where David released his soul into the arms of God and found perfect rest. The presence of his Lord was evident in everything around him. From the coolness of the grass beneath his feet to the sweetness of the streams that calmly wound on their way to the protective trees shading him from the glare of the noonday sun. Truly, this was God's sitting room, and he, David, had been invited as a pampered guest.

And so he did the only thing he could think of to show his gratitude to his gracious host. David played Him songs of worship. He poured out his heart to the Lord, singing of His goodness and His glory. Songs of love and adoration filled the air. Even the birds stopped to listen and bow their heads in agreement. This was life at its best. What his other brothers deemed as tedious work and avoided, he gladly embraced, viewing the hours spent tending sheep as a precious rendezvous with God. Perhaps the Lord had indulged David because He knew of the times that were set before him—times when he would valiantly fight giants and foreigners alike for the freedom of his people. When he would be pursued for years and dodge death at the hands of a paranoid, schizophrenic king. When matters of state, palace intrigue, mounting family pressures, and people around him jostling for position would all overshadow those serene days when he had answered to only one voice...the voice of the Lord. David arched back his neck, welcoming the warm rays from above, and breathed out, "Thank God for those times!" They were a million miles removed from praying on the rooftop of the palace. How many times had he perused the countryside from his bedroom window, mulling on those moments of fellowship that now had to be snatched in bits and pieces from the day's demands?

It was not that God had moved away but rather that he, David, felt the distance widening as the pull of the world around him separated him from that former closeness. But now, as he stood looking at the direction from whence he had come, the palace now completely out of view, his heart rose up within him. *Thank You for the reminder, God, that though my present circumstance seems dire, yet will I praise You. I know who You are. I've seen You. I've heard You before. I know how sweet life can be with You and You alone. And when all is said and done, nothing compares to You. How I thirst for You! How I long to feel Your embrace in the wind. To feel Your touch in the sun. To see Your eyes twinkle in the starlight. This I've grown to appreciate because I've experienced it all, Lord. And nothing—not riches, not fame, not the most beautiful women or the most priceless possessions—compares to You. One moment with You is far sweeter than a lifetime of acquisitions.*

Do you remember when your relationship with the Lord was new? How you couldn't wait to steal away and spend time with Him? Every moment was richly treasured, and then the business of doing God's work took over. The passion that was once directed toward God became diverted to the tasks at hand. Things like this happen. We all make mistakes. We crash and burn. We find ourselves alone again, far from the fickle masses. And then we look upward with a new perspective, realizing that all the things we fight and scrape for are not important at all. And we remember that the most important thing in life is what it was from the beginning...our relationship with our Heavenly Father.

> *Dear Heavenly Father, thank You for always offering cooling streams when our hearts have grown parched from the heat and pressure of all the external affairs that surround us. Sometimes doing distracts us from being who You made us to be— worshipers. Help me to remember, above all things, that as I pursue You and bring pleasure to Your heart, You will guard my affairs and make even my enemies to be at peace with me. Help me to remember that the true place of refreshment and completion is before Your throne. During times when I feel a hunger and a thirst that nothing else seems to fill, help me to have the presence of mind to understand that it is You who my soul really craves. Fill me and satisfy me with Yourself once more. In Jesus' name, amen.*

Weary Times

*When he came to Beersheba in Judah,
he left his servant there, while he himself went
a day's journey into the desert. He came to a broom tree,
sat down under it and prayed that he might die.*

1 KINGS 19:3,4

Elijah was tired. So tired that he was too tired to even vocalize the feeling. There were no words to express this degree of consuming exhaustion. *Where was his reward in serving God?* he wondered. Was this the thanks he got for standing up to the prophets of Baal? For making a mockery of their so-called god? He could still remember the absolute incredulity that came over their faces when God's fire fell and consumed the sacrifice he had prepared for Him. The fire had consumed everything—the sacrifice, the wood, the stones, the soil, even the water in the trench that had been dug around it. That was all the people needed to see to fall on their faces and worship God. Incensed against the prophets of Baal, the crowd rose and slaughtered them all. And then Elijah had prophesied an end to the drought in the land. As the rain fell, Elijah, overtaken by the power of the Lord, ran ahead of Ahab's chariot all the way to Jezreel.

You would think that with all these supernatural manifestations of God's Spirit at work, Elijah would get a little respect. But *nooo*, that evil queen Jezebel had the nerve instead to threaten his life! Her spirit of oppression spread throughout the land, gripping everyone with fear, including her husband, who yielded to whatever she wanted for fear of being confronted by her wrath. And now Jezebel was infuriated at the death of her lackeys, those false prophets of Baal she surrounded herself with. And her undesirable attention was now vindictively directed toward Elijah. Needless to say, this seriously dampened his exhilaration of calling down fire and rain from heaven. His victory felt short-lived as he ran for his life. He felt so isolated, so spent, so...depressed. How God could leave him at the mercy of this wicked woman was beyond him. Why hadn't God struck her down while He was on a roll? After all, Elijah had confronted God's enemies and wiped them out with a vengeance. Didn't one good favor deserve another?

And yet here Elijah was, fleeing for his life. Perhaps he was getting old. Maybe he couldn't take all this excitement anymore. With resignation closing in around him like heavy velvet curtains, he concluded he might as well die—he had definitely had enough. He was too tired to be startled by even the angel of the Lord who appeared to him, instructing him to eat. Almost in a dreamlike state, Elijah did as he was told, eating enough to strengthen himself to make the journey to Horeb, the mountain of God, driven by nothing more than the desire to get some sort of answer.

And then He was there...God, asking Elijah why *he* was there. How could God ask such a question? Didn't He know how hard Elijah had been working for Him? Didn't

He know how badly the rest of the people were behaving? How they had persecuted and killed everyone who made a stand for God? Why, Elijah was the only one left. The only one who hadn't compromised his standards. The last one…and now they were trying to kill him!

He didn't know what to expect as the Lord invited him to stand in His presence on the mountain. At this point, facing the great and powerful wind that tore the mountain apart as well as the earthquake and fire that followed was better than facing Jezebel. But then came the gentle whisper of God, humbling him and asking once again, "What are you doing here, Elijah?" But Elijah missed the real question. "How could you ever feel alone after I've revealed My presence to you in such undeniable ways? Will you always need a major display to be convinced that you're not alone? Don't you know I'm bigger than the box you've put Me in? Don't you know that I am nearer to you in the stillness than I am in all outward manifestations? No, My son, you are not alone. You have reinforcement beyond what your eyes see and your senses conceive. You should have learned that lesson when you were waiting for Me to send the rain."

As Elijah descended from the mountain, reenergized, refocused, reassured, he felt renewed purpose. He had work to do. It was amazing the difference a conversation with God could make. How kind He was, always faithful to meet those who called out to Him at their point of need. Not only did He offer food for the body, He gave fortification to the soul.

*It is the One who is within us that the
enemy hates. Therefore, an attack
against us is an attack against God,
and He takes it personally.*

How many times have you become weary of well doing when you
see no immediate rewards in sight? We struggle even more when we
suffer for righteousness' sake—especially when God doesn't seem to
come against our enemies the way we feel He should. We can stand
in bold, unwavering faith one moment and plummet to the depths
of despair and doubt in a matter of seconds once the enemy of our
souls rises up to retaliate against us. And we begin to take the spiritual warfare that ensues personally instead of remembering that we
never stand alone. It is the One who is within us that the enemy
hates. Therefore, an attack against us is an attack against God, and
He takes it personally. For this reason we have His promise that He is
able to keep that which is committed to Him, for God defends His
own. In that promise we can rest secure that no weapon the enemy
fashions against us will ever prosper.

> *Dear Heavenly Father, in the middle of the fray it is
> easy to lose sight of Your arm defending me and
> Your hand sustaining me. When I hunger, feed me
> with Your Word. When I thirst, refresh me with Your
> Spirit. When I shiver in fear, warm me with Your
> consolation. Make Yourself more real to me than
> You've ever been when I wander alone in the wilder-
> ness. Remind me that when the arrows fly, my rela-
> tionship with You will be my breastplate shielding
> me from Satan's attacks against my heart. Help me*

to constantly practice Your presence even when You
are silent. Train me to hear Your whisper and walk
in the unwavering confidence that You are with me
always. In Jesus' name, amen.

Yielding Times

But the LORD provided a great fish to swallow Jonah,
and Jonah was inside the fish three days and three nights.

JONAH 1:17

Jonah had a sinking feeling that his stubbornness and rebellion had finally caught up with him. From the time God had told him to go to Nineveh, things had taken a turn for the worse. How could God ask him to go to Nineveh? *Nineveh*, of all places! Why should he even bother with those wicked people? Why give them a chance to repent? As far as he was concerned, they weren't even worthy of the chance to receive God's grace. They should be wiped out with one fatal swoop of God's arm. That would serve them right, and still be far too kind an act in Jonah's estimation. They were the most cruel, godless, horrific people on the face of the planet. And where they lived was a literal cesspool of filth and corruption. "Anything goes" was the mantra of Nineveh. Prostitution, witchcraft, murder in broad daylight. People just stepped over the dead bodies and kept on walking, unaffected by it all. These people were known for impaling on poles the heads of those they considered their enemies and parading them around for public sport.

And this is where God wanted him to go to call the land back to repentance? *Thanks a lot, God!* Jonah thought. He was literally being cast to the wolves. If that's as much as God thought about him, perhaps it was time Jonah took his life into his own hands. He was sorry, but no way was he going to risk his neck delivering a message to a scary bunch of people he didn't like anyway. With his luck, they would kill him and *then* repent. And God, being as softhearted toward the contrite as He was, would then turn and pardon them. Oooo, the very thought made Jonah grind his teeth. No way! Absolutely not! God had asked him to do some difficult things in his lifetime, but this was one time he just could not go along with the program.

Of course, who can run from the voice of the Lord and expect anything to go right? Yet Jonah was willing to test his tether. He thought perhaps God had let him off the hook because he was actually able to get on a boat headed to Tarshish. But it didn't take long to find out that God was quite serious about this Nineveh assignment. All of a sudden anxious hands roughly awakened him from a deep sleep. Awakened him to a real nightmare. "Wake up and call on your God. Perhaps He can save us!" someone cried out. The ship was being tossed to and fro on the sea like a balled-up piece of paper. Everyone was in a state of distress, babbling and calling out to whichever god they knew. At a time like this, who could be fussy? Whatever might work, they were willing to give it a try. They were throwing things overboard, and the entire place was up for grabs. In the midst of confusion, Jonah thought to himself, *All right, Lord.*

Jonah knew and the people on board knew that this whole mess was his fault. They had instinctively hesitated to allow him to sail with them when he had mentioned he was running from his God. After all, who had ever succeeded in such an undertaking? But Jonah had convinced them that his God only punished the guilty, and now here they were suffering on his account. But they would not jump to conclusions; they would instead cast lots and find out exactly who had brought all this trouble upon them. Upon Jonah's suggestion that he be thrown overboard, they did not want to appear too hasty. And so they resorted to their own human efforts to row the boat back to shore. Finally having to admit defeat, they reluctantly acquiesced to throwing Jonah overboard, and the sea resumed its calm.

Above on the ship, a fear of the Lord arose and the people blessed God and made a sacrifice to Him. Beneath the ship, sinking deeper into the sea, Jonah could do nothing but grudgingly admit to himself that this was another fine mess he had gotten himself into. Squirming in disgust as he was swallowed by a fish the Lord had prepared, he wondered if this wasn't some sort of cruel joke. Couldn't God just cut him a break? Why did He have to be so stubborn about this Nineveh thing? Well, two could play at this game. And so he sat in the dank belly of the fish and pouted...one, two, three days before beginning his dialogue with God. Knowing he was in no place to argue with God at this moment, Jonah finally conceded, "All right, who am I fooling? You and You alone are God. My fight with You is fruitless. My stubbornness has become an idol I've clung to, separating me from Your grace. You alone have the ability to save even me, O Lord. Here I sit with no power to redeem myself. Only You can do it. I was foolish to withhold my obedience from You; instead I should be offering You a song of thanksgiving for the privilege of being able to serve You." And once God saw that Jonah knew who was boss, He released him to carry out His initial order. He prophesied destruction to the city.

Much to the annoyance of Jonah, God did exactly what he thought He would do. The Ninevites panicked, proclaimed a fast, repented, and God forgave them! "Can you believe that?" Jonah mused. "He allows me to be thrown overboard and swallowed up in a fish for much less than the horrible things these people have done. And they simply cower once and He forgives them, just like that! How could God play me like that? Doesn't He know I could have been stoned for delivering a false prophecy to these people? I just don't get it. He doesn't let me get away with anything! And all around me everyone else gets away with murder. It's better for me to just die right now because this is a losing battle."

And so Jonah sat outside the city and waited...waited to see if God would do His own thing or go along with Jonah's program. After all, he did have a reputation to maintain here. But God had something greater in mind than Jonah's reputation that had nothing to do with his personal worth. This was not a contest between the righteousness of Jonah and the unrighteousness of the Ninevites, or between validating points of view, or even between rewarding the right and punishing the wrong. It was about addressing a need—a need for redemption. God was about the business of bringing thousands of people to the saving knowledge of what Jonah already knew. And like a wise father, He knew His child would understand later but for now He had to do what He had to do. And Jonah must learn obedience for obedience's sake.

What idea of yours have you thought God should go along with lately? I remember that when my brother Ian was very young, every Sunday evening Ford Motor Company ran a television commercial announcing, "Ford has a better idea!" My little brother would get so excited. He would start jumping up and down rejoicing, "Mommy, mommy, Ford has a quacky idea!" No matter how much we tried to correct him, he insisted that Ford had a *quacky*, not a better, idea. Like Ian, sometimes we feel that our ideas are better than God's design, and well, that's just plain ol' quacky. We get indignant, outraged, even downright self-righteous when we don't see others getting the punishment we think they deserve. And then God takes it one step further by suggesting that we *love* those who we don't approve of! Oh, the gall of it all! Doesn't He see what we see? We see so little of the big picture from our vantage point, and perhaps that's why we are limited to a "point of view."

But God has a better idea because He knows the end of the movie. As we make judgment calls based on what our flesh feels rather than what the Spirit of God sees, we struggle to change the storyline to accommodate our own happy ending. This is when the situations of life swallow us up and we hit bottom. We lie there writhing in our own refusal to cry "Uncle," hoping that God will give in. But He doesn't, and we feel forsaken. We mistake His lack of yielding to our program as a lack of love or understanding, and in His eyes one has nothing to do with the other. He simply knows what's best for all involved and refuses to limit the opportunity for all to partake of His grace.

> *Dear Heavenly Father, help me to remember that I*
> *am the child and You are the Father. Help me to*
> *yield to Your loving instruction, being obedient even*
> *when I don't fully understand Your heart. Help me to*
> *move in the quiet trust that You know what is best*
> *for all. In spite of my own preconceived ideas and*
> *prejudices, help me to always keep Your kingdom,*

versus my personal world, in view. Help me to remember that the same grace You now extend to others, You first extended to me, and it is only because of the blood of Your son Jesus that I am counted worthy. There are no works of which I can boast that would suffice to pay for my redemption. Help me to rejoice in Your kindness toward others, understanding that Your love for them does not displace me, as Your love for me does not displace them but rather adds another thread to the tapestry of Your intricate, divine design for Your kingdom. In Jesus' name, amen.

Oh, Lord
Some things You speak
are too profound to share,
too sweet to repeat…
How I revel in our intimacy,
this our secret place
where You whisper things
for my spirit only to hear.
I find my delight
in the knowledge
that we are
co-spirators of Your plan.

Pondering Times

*But Mary treasured up all these things
and pondered them in her heart.*

LUKE 2:19

Although nothing had changed outwardly, Mary stood poised as if contemplating what type of posture she should now assume. How should she walk and talk? Would she feel anything when the Holy Spirit came upon her and the power of the Most High overshadowed her? How should she respond? What should she do? Would it be obvious to others what had taken place? Or was this all just a dream? No, it was real. She touched her face. Yes, it was real, the angel was real. She was fully awake, and she could still recall the angel's words: "You are highly favored! The Lord is with you." What had she done to warrant this type of attention from the Lord? Why was she deserving of so great an honor? To be the mother of the Son of God...the Son of God! She caught her breath at the thought. She dared not speak of this. How could such a thing be verbalized? How could it make any sense in the finite mind of human understanding? Speaking of finite understanding, how would she explain this to Joseph? This matter she would have to leave in the hands of God.

A strange mixture of sorrow and joy flooded Mary. Awe in the face of being called into such a precious place of service to the Lord. Fear as she considered the monumental task. How does one raise the Son of God? How would she prepare this child for God-only-knows what? Truly though He was her son birthed from her body, He would belong to the world. This was a child she would have to love with open hands, being ready and willing to release Him at any given moment. Even now, the protectiveness of a mother's heart quivered at the thought of losing a part of herself. As she traveled to see her cousin Elizabeth, she continued to ponder this matter within herself.

And then there was Elizabeth, shouting to her the most remarkable greeting, confirming what the angel had told her! How did her cousin know? Had the angel told her, too? On second thought, Mary was glad! Relief flooded over her that at last here was someone with whom she could share her soul. Someone who wouldn't think her mad. She took solace in this and waited for God's promise to unfold.

And unfold it did. Joseph too was visited by the angel. He protectively rose to the occasion by taking Mary to be his wife, but still there remained a part of her that couldn't tell him everything she was feeling. Something kept parts of her wandering in the safety of her own spirit about exactly what was to come.

Then the decree came for a census to be taken, and the timing couldn't have been worse. It was late in the hour of Mary's pregnancy and the hard journey became even more arduous as her labor began. After searching every nook and cranny of Bethlehem for a hotel with a vacancy, the stable where they finally camped seemed a welcome haven. Though a stable seemed totally inadequate for the entrance of a king into the world, this was the best they could do given the circumstances. The sounds of the animals were actually soothing in contrast to the jostling crowd that had grown harsh and impatient from waiting in too many lines after too many hours of strenuous travel. No one had a comforting word for anyone, pregnant or not. So it was under the watchful eye of a barnyard audience that the promised Son of God was born.

Funny, He looked just like any other ordinary baby. He was beautiful and new, soft to the touch, delicate and wonderful. A most beautiful child—but then again, every mother thought her child to be the most beautiful of all. And then the strangest thing happened. Shepherds began to come, bearing stories of angels appearing to them in the fields, proclaiming the birth of a Savior! They came to see for themselves this miracle come to earth. Mary's heart trembled within her. It was beginning already. The child she longed to clutch to her breast and never let go of had not been born for her benefit, but instead for the sins of the world. How could she shelter and protect something that was bigger than herself and her husband? Even at this moment, His appearance would forever change her life, and deep within her she knew that this was just the start. Shepherds and kings alike came bearing gifts of adoration for this little infant. Her little infant. What would the future hold? Mary didn't know. So while her heart searched for answers that were yet to be revealed, the visitors mistook her pensiveness for a look of serenity. But inside her heart was beating with a fervency as she turned her eyes toward heaven in a quiet plea, "Lord, I know that He is yours. But grant me a season to love Him as only a mother can, for my heart is woven around this precious gift that You have given and I fear it would break if it were forced to open too quickly. Help me to love the world as much as You do so that I will be willing to share in Your sacrifice."

What has God called you to do? Sometimes the enormity of God's plan in our lives can be overwhelming. It surpasses the furthest stretches of our imagination. And yet He visits us and plants things in our spirit that we know will bring us the greatest joy, but not without experiencing the pain of growth and sacrifice. In those moments it is hard to express the mixture of emotions and questions that swirl to the surface of our hearts. And so we wait for God to unfold the story, almost fearful to look as He turns the pages of our days, humbled that He has called us to a destiny that is so much greater than us.

> *Dear Heavenly Father, when I think of all that You have planned for my life, I stand in silent awe. I am amazed that You continue to be faithful to Your plan for my life even when I am faithless. I thank You that when You make the commission, You make the provision that I may be fully equipped to carry out Your will. Help me to serve You with open hands, always yielding, always releasing, that which You put in my hands back to You. Let my first thought be to glorify You in all that I say or do. In Jesus' name, amen.*

Questioning Times

When John heard in prison what Christ was doing,
he sent his disciples to ask him, "Are you the one who
was to come, or should we expect someone else?"

MATTHEW 11:2

he dankness of the dungeon chilled John the Baptist to the bone. Though he was used to the discipline of fasting, he was hungry and faint from thirst. Yet perhaps the strain he felt was not physical but spiritual. It was as if Herod's fear of him mingled with the hatred of his wife Herodias and permeated the clammy walls of his jail. The question of what should be done with this bold, uncompromising prophet was a touchy question, one that left the air thick with impenetrable tension. Herod was afraid to touch him even though John's condemning comments about his taking his brother's wife frustrated him. He hoped that his arrest would quiet and pacify Herodias. But Herodias could not silence the voice in her head that kept reminding her that she would burn in hell for her sins. For her, the only way to regain peace was to snuff out John's voice once and for all. While she seethed, she considered her options. Why, if she had her way, she would have John the Baptist's head on a platter!

All this, mixed with rumors of what was being discussed beyond the walls of his bondage, began to penetrate even John's reserve of faith. What was wrong with this picture? He had seen Jesus, seen the heavens open and heard the voice of God saying, "This is my son in whom I am well pleased." He himself had confirmed that this was the Son of God. One much greater than himself. He was not worthy to even stand in His presence, and yet after all was said and done, his present reality rocked him, leaving a crack in his heart for some very real concerns to be aired. John was beginning to wonder if he had made a mistake in his judgment. How could he be in this predicament after all that he had done for God? How could his life be left to the hands of those who hated God and scorned His purposes? No less a befuddlement was the lack of response to his crisis from Jesus Himself. After all, not only was Jesus the Son of God, they were relatives! Jesus was his cousin. This was not the behavior he expected from One who was supposed to be a Savior.

How could Jesus go His way and leave John in this dangerous predicament? He thought they had a close relationship. That they had bonded in an even deeper way on the banks of the Jordan. That they were connected. He knew that if the tables were turned, he would be there for Jesus. He would be outside the palace raising havoc, inciting the people to rally behind his demands for the release of Herod's captive. But no one came except his own band of followers, whispering through the bars that separated him from the outside world that, in spite of his present circumstance, God was with him.

Was He really? John couldn't help but vocalize it now to one of his disciples, "Go and ask Jesus if He is really the

One I was looking for to come, or if we should look for another." And then he lowered himself back down to the floor, his heart in a state of torment, torn between what his spirit knew to be true and the facts his mind wrestled to make sense of. He knew from the beginning that he was merely a conduit of the truth which God wanted to convey to this generation. He knew that One greater than himself would come.

He knew that he would have to decrease and Jesus increase. These were his own words that he had spoken to his own disciples who were unsettled by Jesus' rising popularity.

And yet perhaps he had not adequately prepared himself for how the story would really play itself out. Perhaps he took it for granted that he would introduce Jesus and then fade into a peaceful existence somewhere communing with God and baptizing a weary soul or two until he passed from this life peacefully in his sleep. His present dilemma was a stark contrast to that daydream. Instead of feeling content, John felt a little sold out. Left behind for dead. He went back and forth in his mind recalling what he knew of Jesus. He knew it was not in Jesus' nature to lack compassion and yet he was confused by His distance at a time when he needed Him most.

Then the reply came. His disciples had found Jesus and questioned Him. His reply was straight to the point, "The blind receive sight, the lame walk, those who have leprosy are cured, the deaf hear, the dead are raised, and the good news is preached to the poor. Blessed is the man who does not fall away on account of Me." So Jesus did know how he was feeling; this was an unexplainable comfort. His circumstances hadn't changed, but just knowing that Jesus knew how he felt meant more than John could say in that moment. His disciples were looking at him strangely, as if seeing him for the first time, as they went on to relay that this was not all Jesus had to say. They hesitated and looked at one another, as if to confirm that they had indeed heard what they were about to convey next. Then in a rush of incredulity, they went on to tell John that Jesus had spoken to the crowd on his behalf telling them that he, John the Baptist, was the Elijah that had been prophesied to come! That among those born of women, there had not risen anyone greater than John—yet the least in the kingdom of heaven was greater than he.

John felt the weight of doubt and fear roll from his shoulders. Suddenly the dark, depressing dungeon looked lighter, no longer foreboding. The light of the Lord had filled him to overflowing and his heart was reconciled in peace to whatever the future held. He had been affirmed with these words from the One who knew most the secrets of his heart. John also understood that he was a part of something greater than himself. More important than life itself. This was about doing whatever was necessary to further the kingdom of God. There was no room here for selfish fears. And in that moment, John knew that he had been invited to share in the suffering of Christ. He knew that Jesus would also face a time when His very life would be laid on the line. How could he expect to experience less than what his Lord would undergo? As all these revelations flooded his spirit, his voice rose in exultant praise almost drowning out the music that was beginning to waft through the air from the palace. Herod was having another one of his famous parties, but the true celebration was in John the Baptist's heart as he flung open his arms to embrace his call and say yes to his destiny.

Where is Jesus when you need Him most? Why does it often seem that when we are in the midst of doing what God has called us to do that Jesus seems to be the furthest from us? As we are stretched beyond our own limitations, burdened with the cares of far too many issues, our own expectation of God's intervention suffers a disappointing blow. We have a tendency to feel betrayed by what we conclude is His distancing Himself from us. But instead He is merely making room for us to see the greater vision, beyond us, beyond Him, beyond all that we hold dear in our preconceived notions. The ultimate truth is that kingdom business requires that we all get over ourselves and be willing to sacrifice all for the sake of God's higher good. Though He gently affirms us along the way as He reminds us of our ultimate purpose, this can be a lonely revelation. The fact that we intellectually have the best of intentions doesn't negate the reality that our flesh recoils at the thought of such selflessness. Yet this is where the greatest joy is hidden in the bowels of sacrifice.

Heavenly Father, in the moments that I feel deserted by You, help me to see Your presence in the midst of the mission. Help me to keep a purposeful heart that exults in decreasing as You increase in my life and the life of others around me. Help me to remember that I was created for Your good pleasure, and in the fulfillment of what You have ordained for my days my joy will be made complete. Give me the heart of a servant, always ready and willing to serve You. I now present my body and all that I am to You as a living sacrifice, longing to prove what is good, acceptable, and perfect in Your glorious will. This is only reasonable after all that You have done for me. I rejoice in being a vessel You can use. Make me one of honor for Your name's sake. In Jesus' name, amen.

Faithful Times

There was also a prophetess, Anna, the daughter of Phanuel,
of the tribe of Asher. She was very old; she had lived with
her husband seven years after her marriage, and then was
a widow until she was eighty-four. She never left the temple
but worshiped night and day, fasting and praying.

LUKE 2:36,37

Anna made her way carefully through the crowd that had gathered, her heart beating with an exhilaration she hadn't known in years. They parted respectfully before her, acknowledging that a prophetess was in their midst. Even before she was able to see the child, she knew that this was the One. This was the child of promise. The One for whom she had prayed for so many years. Her eyes misted as she contemplated the goodness of God. How kind He was to keep His vow. He had revealed that He would send one who would be the Redeemer. And she had prayed that her eyes would see the consolation of those who mourned beneath the weight of their sins. And now, finally, here He was, this dear sweet child, resting in the arms of this young, beautiful girl who could not possibly begin to fathom the greatness she bore. Nor the pain that would pierce her heart in years to come. But for now this mother gazed lovingly at this gift from God and reveled in being the comfort of the One who would give comfort to the world.

Tears streamed from Anna's eyes as she wordlessly drew nearer to see the infant. It was definitely Him all right. Her spirit leapt within her. How long she had waited for this day! She clutched her breast and thought back to the wonder of being a new bride, the pain of being a widow seven years later, and how she had sought solace in the Temple, held in the arms of God. There she remained from that time to the present, fasting, praying, and worshiping her Lord day and night. And God met her there, telling her things in secret that she shared aloud with all who would listen. This was her life, seeking the face of God. Diligently pursuing Him. And now this was her reward. To see the Word of the Lord in living flesh, right here in this very temple where she had received the promise that He would come.

She never doubted for one moment that what God had said was true. She had only wondered if she would live to see it, and now here was the completion of His Word! The people gathered looked at Anna expectantly, searching for confirmation of what the old man Simeon had said. All respected her as a true prophet of God. Was this tiny child indeed destined to cause the falling and rising of many in Israel? What was the significance of this? But all Anna could do was praise God. After emptying her soul in thanksgiving, she turned to proclaim all that she knew about this marvelous child. Yes, He was the One who would bring redemption to many. She began to unfold all that God had told her in times spent with Him in prayer, gently telling those gathered that they, too, could benefit from more time spent with Yahweh. For as she related these things to them, she realized anew the richness of her life.

She imagined that others probably looked at her as a woman who had fallen prey to unfortunate circumstances. She had become a widow at such a young age, with no kinsman to redeem her, no children to support her, left to depend on the care of the Lord alone. But Anna had never experienced this deep sense of loss that everyone else around her assumed she had felt. So as her married friends retreated out of their discomfort, lacking the right words to say, not knowing how to offer her relief from her pain, Anna sought solace from the only One who knew how to be a comforter to her—God Himself. In His presence, her pain vanished, her burdens were minimized, and she felt a fulfillment that even her loving husband had not been able to give her.

Her days became filled with the expectancy of God meeting her. Imparting things to her that would fill her spirit to overflowing with praise, adoration, and a sense of awe at His marvelous works. Few had this privilege, to walk with God day in and day out, completely undisturbed by the demands of the outside world and necessary routines. She treasured these times, knowing that God had made special provision for her. He was a true Husband to her in every sense of the word. But Anna mourned for her people. She grieved that no true prophet had risen up in the land as in years before when men like Elijah, Samuel, and Nathan had proclaimed the Word of the Lord to the people and even displayed God's great power through mighty signs and miracles. She longed for the day when God would manifest His presence in this way again. As she cried out before the Lord, He surrounded her with His peace and revealed His plan. Her one request had been to see it come to pass. At this He was silent, but she dared to hope He would extend that grace to her. Years passed, and again she asked God if she would see the desire of her heart come to pass. She knew that many others before her had prayed the same prayer and had gone to sleep without seeing the fruition of their requests. So though she dared to hope, dared to dream, dared to pray one more prayer, she silenced her doubts while yielding to God's decision. And now here she was, standing before the manifest Word of God, come to earth in living flesh. She agreed with Simeon, "Lord, you may now dismiss your servant in peace, for my eyes have seen your salvation…"

What is the desire that you have been holding inside of your heart? What are the things that have caused you to grow weary in your faith? The old folks used to say, "He may not come when you want Him, but He's right on time." Isn't it amazing how you can pray and pray for something, the years roll by, and you begin to think that perhaps this is your desire and your desire alone? Did God ever agree with your prayer request? Are you praying in vain? How long should you continue to pray about this? Is your revisiting of this matter evidence of a lack of faith on your part? Why does this thing rest so heavily upon your spirit although you see no sign of God's hand moving to put the wheels in motion? Yet something compels you to keep on persistently putting God in remembrance of this most crucial request. And then one day, out of the blue, the break-through comes! On a day like any other day, you awaken ready to go about your routine and voilá! The deliverance of your expectation greets you, and you are overwhelmed by the faithfulness of God. Perhaps you had even forgotten to pray about it for awhile after exhausting your efforts. But God has not forgotten. And how perfect His timing is, as you realize that *now* is the perfect time for the answer to arrive. How does God do that? He's never a day early, never a day late!

Dear Heavenly Father, help me to wait on You as I look for the fulfillment of my prayers. Bring to my remembrance that my expectation comes from You. Keep me that I may not grow weary of making my requests known to You when I become distracted by impatience. Teach my heart to trust in You, understanding that You know the perfect time to deliver Your promise. As I rest in the knowledge that You do all things well, and that every good and perfect gift comes from You, increase my hope and help my unbelief. But most of all, when the gift arrives, keep me in remembrance of the One who sent it, that I may not love the gift more than the Giver. In Jesus' name, amen.

Expectant Times

*When the disciples were together, with the doors
locked for fear of the Jews, Jesus came and stood
among them and said, "Peace be with you!"*

JOHN 20:19

$\mathcal{W}$as it the chill in the air or their fear that made them tremble? Although they'd had many disagreements about the events of the past few days, they were willing to put their quarreling aside now to draw comfort from one another. Perhaps it was true that there was strength in numbers. While the world churned around them outside, rehashing how the peoples' opinion had suddenly flip-flopped from crowning Jesus king to screaming mad-dening cries of, "Crucify him!" His disciples hid from the public, fearful of their reception from the masses. Would they be next? Would the people want to crucify them too?

But much deeper questions burned in their spirits. This was not the way the disciples had seen the story being played out as they walked with this great Rabbi, watching Him perform awesome miracles. How did someone go from opening blind eyes, unstopping deaf ears, making the lame leap, even casting demons out of the possessed and oppressed...how did someone with this much power end up hanging on a cross? Jesus was dead. This was still sinking painfully into their consciousness. It shamed them to know that someone outside of their inner circle of twelve had seen to His dead body being lowered and then carried away to be buried. They had been too apprehensive of the repercussions of claiming the body. It all seemed so surreal. If He could save everyone else, why wasn't He able to save Himself? Why couldn't He have just concentrated on delivering them from the hands of the Romans? Then this wouldn't have happened. And where was His body now? Had Mary really seen Him? Or were her ramblings about Him rising from the dead—along with Peter and John's—merely delusions from grief? All they knew was that their Lord was gone, and though they were together, they were very much alone.

He had tried to tell them, but they had understood too late. Snatches of conversations now came back like nostalgic whispers, making their grief all the more unbearable. All His talk about leaving that no one ever wanted to take seriously. The whole thing about the bread being His body and the wine being His blood. Tearing down the temple and rebuilding it in three days. What was that all about? Was that another metaphor for Himself? How could such a thing be possible? And why did He have to talk in riddles so much? Why didn't He just make it plain? They couldn't even believe it when He said that one among them would betray Him! Who would ever do a thing like that? After being in His presence, how could any evil remain in your heart? Yet Judas had betrayed Him. What kind of insidious plot had been brewing under their noses? What would make Peter, who loved Jesus dearly, deny Him three times? He was far too bold for that. Everything was just too bizarre. He had warned them that they would scatter and leave Him alone, and they had. It was as if their lives had careened out of control like a bad nightmare, and now they had all awakened, drenched in sweat, with a million questions screaming from every cell within them. And the only One who could answer them was gone. He was gone, and the vacuum He had left in their souls was as vast as the endless desert. They saw no relief from their mourning in sight. How could they ever recover from this?

Their eyes were dark with emptiness, red-rimmed from weeping. Their shoulders slumped in hopeless exhaustion. The women served them soundlessly. They ate without looking at their food. Without looking at each other. Lost in their own thoughts. Trying to sort through the maze of information was impossible, for nothing made sense. Their emotions ran the gamut from fear to doubt to mini sparks of hope that perhaps He really had risen and would show up at any moment to grant them all relief. What were they waiting for? They knew not. They only knew that this could not possibly be the end of the story. It felt too...anti-climactic.

And then, "Peace be with you!" They heard His words before they saw Him. In that instant it was as if someone had rolled away the stone that blocked the light of hope from entering their hearts. It was as if rain had fallen, drenching their parched spirits. It was as if the shackles of weariness had melted away, releasing their prisoners to rejoice again. Peace was with them. Jesus was with them. He was their peace. They breathed in His essence, His breath, and felt their souls come alive. They reveled in the moments He shared with them for the next forty days. Now they learned what they had refused to receive before, walking in a new soberness, finally understanding the season of their visitation. Laying down their own personal agendas, they embraced His plan, finally getting a glimpse of the big picture. Still not having all the answers yet knowing more than before, they now hungrily absorbed all He gave, until at last He departed in a glorious display before their very eyes, this time leaving no doubts in His wake.

As they gathered in the Upper Room to await the One He promised, the atmosphere was drastically different from their first shut-in. This time they felt a spirit of anticipation. There was an electric charge in their midst as they determined their plans to further the gospel and spread the word that Jesus had indeed risen from the dead and would come again for all who believed. The grief of uncertainty now gave way to a sense of new purpose. A refreshing. The disciples remembered the outline Jesus had given them for prayer, and they prayed continually, watching and waiting for the One who would come. Now the only question was *when*.

Suddenly they heard the sound of a mighty wind. This was unusual, for no windows were open. And then cloven tongues of fire descended! They touched each and every one who was gathered. As each was touched, they were filled to overflowing with praise to the Lord. It could not be contained. It bubbled up from their bellies, filling their inner man, bursting forth from astonished lips. Unable to stop the flow, they burst from the room, each proclaiming the goodness of God in diverse languages as the Spirit of the Lord gave these unlearned tongues clear utterance. Would God's wonders ever cease? Even the most reserved was boldly proclaiming the Good News. What a difference the presence of the Lord made! From darkness to light! From fear to faith! From denial to proclamation! From apathy to unbridled passion for the things of God! Their minds had been renewed, their lives transformed forevermore, their expectancy come to fruition, empowering them to proclaim the name of the One they no longer needed to see in order to sense His presence.

What are the areas in your life in which you feel the Lord has left you alone? We've all experienced times in our lives when we wonder where Jesus is. We feel abandoned, paralyzed by our own lack of understanding. Where did we go wrong? When did we miss the turn? It seems as if we have misinterpreted His intentions toward us and now we don't know how to complete the puzzle without His help. So we wait for Him, and the wait is excruciating. But the wait is needed to get rid of us and to make room for Him. To make room for what He wants. His purposes. His plans for us. His gifts that He has deposited in us. His kingdom agenda. So wait we will until our will dies and all that's left within us is the desire to embrace Him and all that He instructs us to do.

> *Dear Heavenly Father, so many times in the past I have superimposed my own desire over Yours. And when I lose You in the midst of all my heart's demands, I return to this place of realizing how desolate I really am without You. Forgive me for my selfishness. Forgive me for assuming that You are here to serve my purposes instead of me serving Yours. Thank You for waiting until I unfold my hands in complete surrender to You. I now release all that I hold dear and choose to grasp only what You offer. Teach me again the things I chose to ignore. Make Your purposes clear to my heart. Remove all fear and doubt from my spirit. Breathe on me once more and revive my soul to pursue its ultimate purpose— proclaiming Your Word in all I say and do for the glory of Your name and the salvation of others. In Jesus' name, amen.*

Yet I am not alone,
for my Father is with me.

JOHN 16:32

Isolated Times

*For I am already being poured out like a drink offering,
and the time has come for my departure. I have fought
the good fight, I have finished the race, I have kept the faith.
Now there is in store for me the crown of righteousness, which
the Lord, the righteous Judge, will award to me on that day.*

2 TIMOTHY 4:6-8

Paul set his pen down beside the parchment and rubbed his eyes. The light was fading...the evening of his life was setting in. He felt as if he had so much more to say in order to prepare everyone for his absence, but he was weary. Weary and ready to go on, yet torn by his own protectiveness toward those he had fathered for so long. Rome, Ephesus, Corinth...the roll call scrolled across his heart. These people were as dear to him as if they were his own children. How he had labored with them! Teaching them precept upon precept, principle after principle. In hindsight his work had not been in vain, though many times his patience had been sorely tested by reports he received of their behavior. But then he'd also hear the reports of fruit abounding, many being added to the church, and the name of the Lord being glorified among the most unexpected sources. This evened the score, and for this Paul was grateful.

Though he had suffered at the hands of some he had helped he did not blame God or presume negligence on His part. He attributed it instead to the mere humanity of even the most godly of men. Paul left the judgment of those who had cruelly failed him in the hands of the One he served. So it was without bitterness that he told Timothy of how no one came to stand with him and offer him support at his last trial, and how it was to God's credit alone that he was not thrown into the lion's den, as was the custom of the day. He stopped and drew comfort from those words. *God is on my side. He has never failed me. I have worked diligently to the end for my Lord. Looking back, in spite of my human failings, I think I did a pretty good job. I fought the fight, I kept the faith in spite of the many hardships I endured. I kept my focus. I was determined to fulfill the purpose that the Lord ordained, called, and set me apart to achieve. I have lived my life on purpose to that end, and I feel I have done what I was supposed to do. This is my consolation.*

And, as it happens to anyone who has done a hard day's work, exhaustion took its toll, heightening Paul's level of sensitivity. Now loneliness seemed more apparent than ever. The walls of his jail cell looked more cold and unwelcoming than before. Luke alone had come to visit him that day, and Paul's heart ached to see those who were close to him. He prayed that Timothy and Mark would hurry to visit. What welcome sights their faces would be. How he missed the warmth and friendliness of the household of Onesiphorus, of Priscilla and Aquila. He missed their cooking, their laughter, and the way they shared their faith in earnest. He missed the simple things, and he recalled these treasured moments of pleasure time and time again to cheer himself in the passing hours of solitude. He felt saddened at the thought of never seeing them again.

This was the part he struggled with from time to time. He had endured many things—beatings, shipwrecks, stonings, being left for dead—but his greatest sorrow was parting from those he carried in his heart. He had to remind himself that God was able to keep them all and carry on without him. It was not his letters of correction that kept them going, but the Spirit of God and their own cooperation with His leading. After all, hadn't all of his pivotal experiences with God taken place just between the two of them with no outside influence or vocal nudgings? Paul's had, for the most part, been a solitary walk with God. And all that God had deposited in him during those times alone, he had turned to pour out to those around him.

His heart burned for all to grasp what he had so voraciously received. Perhaps he was hungrier than most, having been so acquainted with the vacuum that worldly learning can leave. It seemed the more knowledge one acquired, the less one knew. Before his conversion, this had made Paul angry when he encountered the Christians. They seemed to be a mirror reflecting that he really knew nothing at all. He mistook their serenity for harbored amusement at his ignorance, their refusal to defend themselves for haughtiness. How dare they think themselves better than he when he had the finest of breeding in every measure! Their security threatened his state of well-being, and so he sought to snuff them out. He wanted to silence their spirits that screamed at him from tranquil faces and haunted him after every unnerving encounter. And that Stephen was the last straw! How dare he have the audacity to gaze calmly into heaven while being stoned! Paul would show these people who was superior! But God chose to have the last word, silencing his rage and filling what had long been empty to overflowing.

And now Paul was hovering protectively over the church he had railed against. He longed for the salvation of the lost, praying they would finish the journey as worthy contenders for the faith. What a long way he had come, and now his journey was winding to an end. This was the test—being ready for that which he spent a major part of his life preparing others to enter into. Repeatedly, the reluctance of leaving those he cherished played tug of war with his readiness to be united with the Lord. Instead of dwelling on the inevitable—for God had never allowed anything to happen in his life without warning—he prepared himself to leave in the only way he knew how. Every key that could help Timothy and the others run the race effectively now poured out of him for the last time. These were not just words; they were his heart poured out on paper. He prayed that they could read between the lines. And as the night chill closed in, Paul wrapped himself in the comfort that God was able to keep all that was committed to Him. In this he found his final release.

Is there someone you are clinging to as a support in your faith? There comes a time in the life of every believer when we must accept the fact that every runner must run alone. None of us is able to bear the weight of another's salvation after all is said and done. This is the time when we find there is One who has been carrying us all along. This silent partner waits to speak only after we surrender our insistence to cling to others.

Dear Heavenly Father, please prepare me for the day when I stand before Your throne alone to give an account of my life. I pray that I will be able to have the same confession that Paul had. That I lived my life on purpose, that I strove daily for the calling of the Most High, for herein lies my true fulfillment. It is my desire at the end of the day to be able to say that I lived a life for Christ. Instruct me in Your ways that I might be effective in the midst of those You send me to, that I might have a list of lives that I've affected, spirits I have nurtured, hearts I've realigned for Your sake, for Your glory. Help me not to glory in the things that I've achieved but in becoming all that You have called me to be for the furtherance of Your kingdom. But most of all, help me to look past all others and find all that I'm searching for in You. In Jesus' name, amen.

Visionary Times

After this I looked, and there before me was a door standing open in heaven. And the voice I had first heard speaking to me like a trumpet said, "Come up here, and I will show you what must take place after this." At once I was in the Spirit, and there before me was a throne in heaven with someone sitting on it.

REVELATION 4:1,2

John was stunned. Not surprised, but stunned. His mind reeled from all that he had seen. He must record every iota. No detail could be left out. Every word had to be guarded like an invaluable gem. Not one word must be added or taken away from what the angel had shown him. These were no delusions from his seclusion; these were revelations that emanated straight from the throne room of God. Warnings of future turmoil, assurances of the victory of Christ, the triumph of the church, and the defeat of the evil one. Truly God was the Alpha and the Omega, the Beginning and the End. John felt as though he had just completely grasped the revelations he had received of what took place in the beginning, and now God was completing the picture with insights of the end. Truly, He was able to complete that which He began, and the proof was in His Word.

For John this was more than he could take in, and he struggled to stand in the face of all that he was shown. How could he ever have imagined the glory Jesus had left behind to live among them? He'd had no real idea of who the man was he had walked and talked with for those three short years. This same humble man who had no specific address. Who boasted of nothing and never insisted on having His own way. Who lowered Himself to levels that even the humblest man would not tolerate. And yet Jesus did all these things because He knew all along who He was. Only those around Him lacked understanding. John had lain his head against this same Jesus' breast and listened to His heartbeat. And now here he was in the throne room seeing his friend, the one he called "Rabbi, friend," clothed in light, bathed in the honor of angels who stood before Him, crying, "Holy!" He was the Lamb of God, exalted above all other names. And none of the other twelve were with him to see the splendor, the power, the might, the majesty, of the One they had eaten with, communed with, and even forsaken.

John was alone, being shown things so unbelievable you had to see them to receive them. Yet he knew these events would unfold just as they were told. That the evil one would wreak havoc against the saints and that the Lamb would prevail. That there would be war in the heavens and on the earth. That world systems would fall and that the power of men would fail. This was the kingdom that Jesus had spoken of while on the earth. Small wonder they were not able to fathom what He spoke of! Truly their eyes had not seen, their ears had not heard. It had not entered into their hearts in even the minutest inkling the things that God had prepared for those who loved Him. This was beyond any of John's wildest expectations. He thought he had grasped the concepts Jesus had shared, but in reality he hadn't come anywhere close in his understanding. Perhaps it was only in isolation that one was capable of seeing Jesus for who He really was.

Now it was all so clear! Everything that Jesus had said now made so much sense! Though in retrospect, after Jesus' departure from earth back to heaven, John had hints of this as he wrote his chronicle of how he understood it all to have begun. This was the cement. Seeing the Father and the Son, witnessing the power of the Spirit of God. "In the beginning was the Word, and the Word was with God and the Word was God." Yes, truly Jesus had been with God in the beginning. The Spirit had given him the revelation of this, for now it was clearly evident. The Three were indeed One, a mystery that could only unfold in its entirety from a personal witness. Now the One he knew as friend, he also knew as King.

John recalled that Paul had spoken of being caught up to the third heaven. He, too, had said the visions and revelations he received from the Lord were so astounding that they could not be told. Now he understood. So obediently John wrote what the angel dictated. He wrote of things fearful and awesome. Majestic and triumphant. Prophetic and revealing. How he longed for the others to see what he was beholding. But the Lord had chosen him to see, to record, to tell. He only hoped that he could capture all the detail in a way that others would understand.

Not knowing how long his exile would last or if he would ever be released to rejoin the others at Ephesus, John rehearsed in his mind all the events he had witnessed over and over until they rang in his heart. Bursting with anticipation for the culmination of these events to come to pass, he prayed the only prayer his spirit could utter after such an experience: "Come, Lord

Jesus." For now every moment apart from Him would seem an eternity.

For it is only through true relationship
and intimate time spent with Him
that we will see Him as He truly is
and acquire the faith we need
to possess His promises to us.

What are the promises of God for your future? Are you listening? When the Israelites stood at the foot of the mountain with Moses and saw the glory of the Lord come down to meet them, they rejected the presence of God out of fear and released Moses to bring them messages back from God. When they forfeited the presence of God, they gave up something greater—the opportunity to see Him not only as an awesome God, but also as a friend. Because of this lack of intimate relationship, it became difficult for them to trust Him. No trust, no entering into the Promised Land. For it is only through true relationship and intimate time spent with Him that we will see Him as He truly is and acquire the faith we need to possess His promises to us. In these times of revealing, He whispers secrets that no man's ears can hear, for only spirits can receive such things. And He waits for an opportune time, when we are far from the crowd, to surround us with Himself and His promises, which are too rich for the undiscerning.

Dear Heavenly Father, sometimes I avoid Your presence out of fear of what You will reveal to me. And then, when I finally get to that place where You have my full attention, the things You share with me are far too wonderful for me to comprehend. I pray that my hunger for You and the words You speak to me increase, for I have found that when I am consumed with Your promises, my joy is full and my faith is overflowing. Continue to draw me to Yourself and show me more and more of You. Prepare me to share what You give with others, that their spirits may be edified and their hope renewed in You. In Jesus' name, amen.

Wilderness Times

Jesus said to him, "Away from me, Satan! For it is written:
'Worship the Lord your God, and serve him only.'"
Then the devil left him, and angels came and attended him.

MATTHEW 4:10,11

he reflective halos were like smoke rings ever broadening as they emanated from the naked, luminous ball that shed light on the desirable as well as undesirable in this wilderness. Squinting from the brilliance of the noonday sun, Jesus tried to distinguish if they were simply mirages shielding something more ominous. He was so hungry, so thirsty...

Something—or was it someone?—cast a shadow over the light, breaking its rays, giving some relief to His burning skin. He looked up, cupping His hands over His eyes to help them adjust, trying to see exactly what it was that had happened upon Him. Aahh, this was a familiar face—Satan! He felt sadness at the sight of this lost and unrepentant soul, but He also felt some righteous indignation as He recalled the revolt this solitary figure had tried to lead against His Father in the heavenlies. This foe He had once called friend had risen to incite one-third of the heavenly host against the throne of God, and He, Jesus, had waged war against him, casting him down. Satan had fallen like lightning from the sky along with the angels he had rallied to his cause, still screaming his threats that he would somehow get back at them all. Supposing he was doing a good job at fulfilling his vow ever since tempting Adam and Eve to fall, Satan now confidently sauntered up to Jesus, a smooth smile doing little to cover the hatred that glittered behind his hooded eyes.

Jesus understood that this man, this entity, this fallen angel who used to gather the praises and present them so magnanimously before His Father, was not one to be trusted. So He gave him no greeting. He was almost hypnotic to take in, however, for he was still quite beautiful, but in a twisted, perverted kind of way. As a matter of fact, he was only beautiful at first glance. If you really looked, you would begin to take in the horrid little imperfections that marred his features in a disturbing way. The longer you stared, the more repulsive he became. It was clear that Satan truly believed his own press and was quite heady with the power he held over this small domain he had been given for only a season. Why, he even had the nerve to try the same manipulation that he had used on others now on Jesus, as if the Son of God were merely some new kid in the neighborhood who was not yet familiar with the town bully's tricks. Jesus almost felt sorry for him. Didn't this fallen one understand that the longings of the flesh could never be fulfilled apart from the Word that God so lovingly gave to His children?

It was almost amusing, that Satan would ask Jesus to prove He was the Son of God by manipulating Him to test His own Father! Didn't he understand this was not about Jesus proving anything to anyone? He knew who He was, and who His Heavenly Father was to Him—that was enough. And the nerve of Satan, to offer Him something that already belonged to Him! The years of separation from God had truly twisted his logic. Had Satan forgotten that he was only the prince of this world and that He, Jesus, was still King of kings and Lord of lords? Well, he would be reminded soon enough. Though Satan rehearsed scripture back to Him, it seemed as if the serpent had developed convenient amnesia, doing anything that worked to get him the results he wanted. And he got rid of anything that would reveal to his chosen victim that his offer was as useless as a bucket of water was to the sea. What could he offer that God couldn't do greater? Absolutely nothing! This Jesus knew on authority. He had this truth straight from the throne room.

And so they stood face to face, yet kingdoms—worlds—apart. One disguised as light, the other emanating pure light, the only difference being their relationship with the Father of Light—God Himself. Though both looked alone, only one was truly alone, separated for all of eternity from the One who gave all that he craved—power, wealth, and fulfillment. Only God could give the ability to gain these things. And only when given from His hands would they be lasting. To acquire these things by one's own devices led to a life of trying to secure one's holdings. This was a hard existence that left one bitter, weary, and disillusioned. But now, sadly, this was the only life that Satan knew. A life filled with attempting to get everyone in the world to see his flawed point of view and to go along with it. Jesus shook His head at all the possibilities that Satan had forfeited in his rebellion. It was His Father's good pleasure to give him the kingdom within the confines of His Lordship, but for Satan that wasn't enough. So now, ultimately, he would have nothing.

Of course, even in the midst of this weak game of bartering, Satan still did not understand what he was dealing with because Jesus' mission was so contrary to Satan's character. He had no concept of becoming nothing in order to gain everything. His pride demanded that he validate his power with an accumulation of praise unto himself. That he flaunt his wares and assets, so to speak. Glorify God? Whatever for? No, Satan had missed the point, but Jesus hadn't. He knew who He was. He knew who His Father was. He understood every facet of their relationship and walked secure in His Sonship. This left no room for His flesh to feel need above and beyond what God had already provided for His spirit. His Father was His Friend; this was all He needed. As He watched Satan depart from Him after He had reminded His lost friend how the scriptures really go, Jesus knew that He would see His foe again. Satan had always been resilient, a sore loser, though his was a losing battle.

As the angels came to minister to Jesus, reviving His strength for what lay ahead, He again reflected on how sad it was that some would choose to go their own way, meandering down the road of self will, only to find themselves alone. How sad it would be for them to find, at the end of the day, that all the things they acquired and accomplished were only cruel traitors robbing them of true and everlasting joy. As He basked in the care of His Father and those He had sent, He rested secure...definitely not alone.

What parts of yourself have you reserved for you and you alone? From the time we burst forth from our mother's womb, the grasping begins. Though we crave the love and security of our parents, we have an even greater desire for control. We cry and that gets us attention. We learn this early and use this newfound knowledge almost immediately to get what we crave. But then our parents begin to set boundaries and we rebel, not recognizing the limits as detours that set us on the right track. We don't realize that we must learn how to yield in order to be blessed. So we fight for our own way and lose the grace that could be ours to help us attain what we truly desire. Our rebellion places a breach in our relationship with God, causing discomfort and even the forfeiture of gifts and privileges. Oh, but the blessings that await the child who grasps his Parent's hand and accepts His leading!

Dear Heavenly Father, far too often I have sought my own way, much to my own personal demise. Help me to understand this unique relationship that You desire to have with me. Give me a personal witness of Your love and Your intentions toward me. Teach me of Yourself and increase my trust in You. Make Yourself and Your Fatherhood real to me and increase my love for You, that I might withhold nothing of myself from You. As I meditate on Your Word, make it come alive on the inside of me. Grant me the revelation of Your heart as I read every line. Let Your Holy Spirit fill me with a passion for Your purposes. I desire to be Your child in every sense of the word, bringing pleasure to Your heart and a smile to Your lips. Help me to be ever aware of Your presence and Your love for me, that I may act accordingly. In Jesus' name I pray, amen.

In the Midst of the Crowd

It is not the ragings of the voices
that surround that one must heed,
but the still small stirrings
that the inner voice creates.

Decisive Times

But Noah found favor in the eyes of the LORD...
Noah was a righteous man, blameless among
the people of his time, and he walked with God.

GENESIS 6:8,9

oah pounded the last peg into the hull of the
ark, closed his eyes, and thanked God. At last it was complete. It had taken him one hundred and twenty years of
steadfast obedience in the face of ridicule, relentless questions, and taunts of disdain to complete this assignment.
"Rain?" some had said, looking at him as if he'd lost his
mind. "What exactly is rain? How can water come from the
sky? It's never come from the sky before. Why should it
come now? And surely it would be impossible for so much
water to fall that it would warrant the building of
this...monstrosity!" They didn't know quite what to call
this colossal ship. When he first began building it, the
onlookers took bets among themselves as to how long it
would take him to abandon this senseless project, but year
after year had gone by and Noah was still diligently

working. His obsession with impending doom had passed from ridiculous, unwarranted fear to dementia as far as they were concerned. All this talk of rain. What foolishness. Everyone knew that the earth irrigated itself from the streams that flowed beneath it. That water would actually fall in torrents from the sky in such massive doses that all of mankind would be destroyed—what an absurd notion!

And on top of that, the nerve of Noah to think that he, along with his family, were the only ones who would escape God's displeasure if He did indeed choose to unleash His wrath upon society. Why couldn't he just live and let live like the rest of them did? All of this talk about God seemed to have a rather damaging effect on his psyche. If that was what walking with God was all about, they could do without this too-strict overseer. They had no time for Noah's doom and gloom. No time for being so prim and proper. Always crossing your spiritual *t's* and dotting your religious *i's* was far too laborious. It just required too much sacrifice and concentration to get this righteous thing down. Noah needed to relax, relate, release. Life was to be embraced fully, freely sampling every pleasure and becoming intoxicated with the fulfillment of your every lust and desire. Looking at Noah's life, they wondered where the reward or fun in righteousness was. If all you got out of pleasing God was getting stuck building a stupid ship for one hundred and twenty years and being the laughingstock of society, they wanted no part of it.

So they drank, made merry, and continued on with their lives, stopping by every now and again to see if Noah had tired of his building project yet. He was included in the sightseeing tour whenever relatives and friends came to visit. "Oh, yes, and you must see our local preacher. He's been building a ship forever! He claims that water is going to destroy us all. Isn't that a scream?" They could always count on Noah to provide a good laugh, at least when he wasn't making them uncomfortable with his convicting forecasts.

One day, Noah and his ark were once again the main topic of discussion at the wedding feast of his neighbor's daughter. Several guests commented on the uncommon darkness of the sky. Thick, dark clouds were rolling across the heavens, leaving angry marks upon the crisp, sparkling blue firmament that had previously promised to serve as the perfect canopy for this afternoon of celebration. It was almost as if God was frowning down upon them and every cloud was another wrinkle in His creased brow. The animals were also behaving rather strangely, someone commented. They seemed…restless, nervous, as if alarmed by something their masters could not see. Flocks of birds soared frantically overhead, back and forth, as if trying to decide in which direction they could escape their invisible pursuer.

And then they felt it. At first it was as if someone had accidentally flicked a drop of water on them. But upon surveying those around them no guilty culprit was found. As a matter of fact, everyone was doing the same thing! They looked in dismay at their garments. One drop. Two drops. Three *large* drops…of water…but coming from where? Slowly their eyes turned upward as they realized indeed that water was falling from the sky. Before this phenomenon could sink in, the water began to descend in sheets, drenching them completely. At first they stood rooted to the spot, incredulous, looking from their cupped hands to the sky as if attempting to connect the water splashing upon them to its source. Finally the reality of the moment sank in. The mad scurrying that ensued as everyone ran for cover was lost on Noah, who was comfortably settled into his ark, closing the cage door on the last animal that had entered. He cast one last sad glance toward the outside world as the Lord shut the door.

"The old man was right!" they screamed, heading blindly in the direction of Noah's ark. "Perhaps he will allow us to come in," they said, ignoring the shame they should have felt for their past cruel comments. But upon reaching the ship, they found the entrance sealed. Their hearts sank with their shoes into the mud. "If this keeps up, we'll all die," they moaned as they leaned against the ship, trying to think of another alternative. And then, horror of horrors, the springs beneath the earth began to burst forth as well! With this the people beat a hasty retreat, deciding that their rooftops were their last resort. Why hadn't they listened to Noah? Who could have known that his ramblings would come to pass? Over the next forty days and nights, the water rose to claim its victims one by one until nothing was left except the ark floating on the face of the waters, carrying its precious cargo.

As the water subsided so did God's anger. Remembering Noah, who had found favor with Him because he never allowed his heart to stray in the direction of the masses, God let the heavens and the earth finally rest. Noah disembarked tentatively from his new home, not knowing what to expect beyond the world he had grown used to. It had been almost a year since he had set his feet upon solid ground. Stillness and serenity greeted him. As far as his eye could see, fresh vegetation was beginning to peek out from its hiding place. Was this what Adam had felt? Then again, Adam had no history to mar his enjoyment of all that God had created. Noah had memories of more grievous days, and he was looking forward to a new beginning. His first thought was to make a sacrifice unto the Lord. Everything else had been swept away, but there was still God. As the pungent aroma of an acceptable offering wafted toward the heavens, God wrote a new covenant promising faithfulness between Himself and all life on earth. Across the sky, His handwriting reflected the prisms of His majesty in the form of a brilliant rainbow. Never again, He promised, would He pour out His wrath in such a devastating fashion. Noah gratefully accepted this promise. And in his mind, the rain that others had looked upon as God's wrath, he actually saw as God's tears—tears shed weeping for a lost world. *Oh, that I might never cause you to weep again,* he thought. And before this inner cry was complete, God added yet another ring to His handiwork, as confirmation of His pledge.

When are you most tempted to go with the crowd, even when you know they are going in the opposite direction of God's plan for your life? "Eat, drink, and be merry today, for there's always tomorrow to get it right," seems to be the mantra of the day for most. Yet there are some of us who God has reserved unto Himself, struggling to maintain lives that will be pleasing to our Lord and King. As sin becomes more and more the norm and doing wrong becomes more of a casual pastime, it's easy to feel like the odd one out. But you're not out there alone. This is the place where God's favor and protection can be found. Like mama always said, every dog has its day, and that is the truth. In God's economy, doing nothing for Him leaves you with nothing in the end. No guarantees of His faithfulness, provision, or protection when the hard times come. You're on your own. But for those of us who stand our ground when everyone else around us is slippin' and slidin', He shuts us in, shields us from the ravages of disobedience, and surrounds us with His peace.

Dear Heavenly Father, when it's hard for me to swim against the tide of popular reasoning, help me to stand fast in my obedience to You. Help me to constantly be transformed by the renewing of my mind. Feed me from Your word with revelation and understanding, but most of all give me a heart that beats for You so that after all is said and done, I will walk in a way that pleases You. Not based on what I know, but Who I know. Not based on fear of the consequences, but based on my love for You. In Jesus' name I pray, amen.

Hateful Times

"Here comes that dreamer!" they said to each other. "Come now, let's kill him and throw him into one of these cisterns and say that a ferocious animal devoured him. Then we'll see what comes of his dreams." When Reuben heard this, he tried to rescue him from their hands. "Let's not take his life," he said.

GENESIS 37:19-21

Reuben was torn. On one hand he could relate to how his other brothers felt. Joseph *was* a spoiled brat, a little too cocky for his liking. If his little brother thought he would ever bow down to him, he had another thing coming! On the other hand, he thought that Simeon and the others were pushing the envelope a bit too far. How could they even speak of killing their own brother? Rough him up and teach him a lesson, maybe. But murder? That was over the top. He felt reluctant to say anything, knowing his brothers all too well. His objections would be met with accusations about Reuben's own questionable character. They would dredge up the whole incident about him sleeping with his father's concubine and end with a crescendo of condemnation, asking him who he was to try to make them feel guilty about anything.

This always made Reuben fold back inside himself, wondering if God would ever grant him an opportunity to redeem himself. He had sinned out of anger and pain. No one else seemed to notice the suffering he had witnessed in his mother's eyes every time his father, Jacob, had glanced lovingly in the direction of Rachel, his other wife. They hadn't watched their mother cry every time his father went into Rachel's tent to be with her for the night. Though his mother, Leah, and Rachel were sisters, all the children they produced were part of a contest, a desperate wager to gain Jacob's affections. As a boy, his mother had even sent him to gather mandrakes so that she might concoct a love potion, an aphrodisiac, to gain Jacob's amorous attention! It was an insult. An insult to his mother. He had seethed throughout his entire childhood.

His father had never felt the pain of being rejected, having something taken from him. He deserved to be hurt so that he could see how it felt. So what if it was a sin and a disgrace for Reuben to sleep with one of his father's women. It was a disgrace how Jacob treated Leah! So he flaunted his youth and virility in the face of Jacob's age. Yet his anger and pain had not subsided after lying in Bilhah's arms. No feeling of release came from the look of distress and hurt he saw in his father's eyes when Reuben's behavior was brought to his attention. As a matter of fact, he felt even more dead than before. He concluded that he had imprisoned himself with his own lack of forgiveness, first for his father, and now for himself. He was not surprised that Joseph would be his favorite son. After all, he was born from Jacob's favorite woman. Reuben had taken the special treatment of his halfbrother in stride, though it often felt like sandpaper scraping across an old wound that was still festering.

As he hurried back to the cistern to retrieve Joseph and send him on his way, Reuben stopped with a start. Where was he? He could just see it now—here was something else he would be blamed for. And indeed he should be. He was the oldest. He should have pulled rank, taking a firmer stand against their abuse of Joseph. But now it was too late. He looked at his brothers with different eyes as they calmly wove their tale of deception about the death of Joseph at the hand of wild animals. Who were these people? How could they sell their own brother into slavery? Was he the only one who had a conscience? They could degrade him, Reuben, as much as they pleased about what he had done in the past; he deserved it. But Joseph did not deserve this. And Jacob did not deserve this either, no matter what type of father or husband he had been. But Reuben went along with their plan, as he did with everything else they did, too weary to go against the flow any longer.

The news broke the old man when they returned home, and it broke something in Reuben that day too. All the anger he felt toward Jacob melted as his father's tears washed away all the residual bitterness that had built up over the years. But still fearing the repercussions, Reuben couldn't bring himself to tell Jacob the truth. Instead he worked out his guilt by extending himself as much as he could toward his father and Joseph's remaining younger brother, Benjamin. During the day he was the consummate caregiver to them. At night he fought his own demons as he experienced consuming nightmares of Joseph being tormented and calling to him. In the dreams he would try to rescue Joseph, but his brother was always out of reach. Time and time again he failed to be his salvation. And therefore he had none of his own.

Years passed and the famine came. They were struck hard, and Reuben felt he'd gotten his just desserts. But off to Egypt they went. He thought of how his brother had long ago gone down this same path as they journeyed past landmarks that reminded him all too well of that day. Upon reaching Egypt all the rest of the events became a swirling maze...snatches of reality breaking through...the tall stranger who seemed oddly familiar yet bore no resemblance to anyone he knew...the accusal of being spies...demanding Benjamin be presented as proof that they were not lying. This was where it had to stop; Reuben couldn't take any more. This time he didn't care what anybody had to say; he was going to take the bull by the horns and take responsibility. If need be, he would offer the lives of his own sons in exchange for Benjamin. This was his last chance to work out his own salvation, to try to silence his brother's blood from accusing him any further. So back to Egypt they went. Again the events blended together...being invited to this Egyptian's house for dinner...being seated in birth order...how did he know?...being accused of stealing!... Oh, would condemnation never feel its work was through? This was a worse nightmare than the one he had been having repetitively. And then the light broke...a moment of redemption more glorious than he ever had hoped for now arrived. Joseph was alive! Alive and well! Alive and well and a man of great influence in Egypt!

Now Reuben was relieved to bow at his brother's feet. Gone was the bile that had risen in his throat when Joseph predicted this moment so long ago. He was free. He felt as if he were being washed by rain as his own tears cleansed his soul and he begged for forgiveness. He would have given any amount of money, time and time again over the years, to be able to go back in time and report to Jacob that his favorite son was alive. To see the smile that came upon the old man's face at news more glorious than even the birth of his first son. The shackles that bound Reuben's soul fell off that day. God had not forsaken him; He had indeed been merciful to release him from his self-inflicted hell. Perhaps his past awful deeds and awful words could not be taken back, but God had extended His grace to him in the only way he could have ever regained his peace—by granting him one more opportunity to bring pleasure to his father's heart. Reuben knew there was only one way—through his son.

What things still burden you from your past? We've all met him and realized from experience that Condemnation is a brutal bully. He paralyzes us when we want to do right by reminding us of our past misdeeds: "Who do you think you are? How dare you get on your high horse after what you've done! Won't you look ridiculous trying to play the saint? *Every*body knows what you're really made of!" That's usually enough to stop us dead in our tracks. Make us compromise standards we've thought better of. Discourage us from correcting someone else, lest our conscience remind us we're no better than they are. We're too busy stoning ourselves to stone the enemy. And yet God waits to exchange our sin and condemnation for the life of His Son. If He can make such a tremendous sacrifice, surely we can release a few bags we no longer need to carry.

> *Dear Heavenly Father, I've done some things in my life that I am so ashamed of. I feel that I might never break free of the accusing voices in my head. I wonder how You could love someone like me and if a second chance can ever be a reality. A clean, fresh start seems to be an elusive dream buried under the burden of my guilt. I struggle to release myself from my guilt, only to find myself sinking deeper into the quicksand of resignation that I will never be able to change. I find myself clinging to one solitary promise.*

He who the Son has set free is free indeed. Father, I reach out my hands to You; meet me in this place of failure. I call on You to free me from my sins. Even greater yet, free me from myself. Wash me, restore me, and help me to begin again. In Jesus' name I pray, amen.

Impatient Times

*When the people saw that Moses was so long
in coming down from the mountain, they gathered around
Aaron and said, "Come, make us gods who will go before us.
As for this fellow Moses who brought us up out of Egypt,
we don't know what has happened to him."*

EXODUS 32:1

To be perfectly honest, Aaron had no explanation for the delayed return of his brother, Moses. He wished Moses had given him some idea of how long he was going to be gone. The masses were restless, and he was getting nervous. He was also growing weary of their constant complaining. They were never satisfied. Perhaps it was a habit they would never break. Aaron didn't know how the Lord felt about it, but he was sick of their attitude. You would think that by now they'd be convinced of the power of God. He had brought them out of Egypt, given them food, water, victory over Pharaoh's chariots...certainly that was enough! As far as he was concerned, God had proven Himself. But then again, the people were afraid of this God. Even Aaron had to admit He seemed a bit fearsome. When He descended to the foot of the mountain to speak with the people, they were afraid of His glory and fled. No longer willing to meet with God, they handed the task of message-bearer to Moses. They forfeited being in the presence of God and enjoying one-on-one communication with Him for secondhand "he said, God said" conversation. And now that Moses had gone to get the message they chose not to receive first-hand, they had the nerve to be upset because he was taking too long! Well, you just couldn't win for losing with these people.

Aaron was annoyed. Annoyed by a lot of things. On one hand, Moses expected him to be a leader on call. On the other hand, Moses was running everything: "Do this, do that." Aaron grumpily muttered under his breath as he reviewed his list of disappointments. By his estimation, his role was not clearly defined. Was he always to repeat whatever Moses told him God said he should say? He wanted to do some thinking for himself, not just carry out a bunch of orders. And that brought him back to his original quandary—Moses had left him "in charge" of these people who seemed to have no respect for anyone, including God. Now that they'd decided that Moses wasn't coming back, they thought they needed to create some other god to lead them. Well, wasn't that just too ironic? They didn't want to talk to the God they had; they merely wanted a more manageable model of Him. One that couldn't talk back. One that let them do as they pleased and blessed them, anyway.

Who was he to argue with these people? Why should he put himself in personal danger, anyway? Moses was the one who was ultimately responsible for them all. Let him deal with them whenever—if ever—he returned. So Aaron ordered all of them to bring their gold earrings to him, and he gave them what they had been asking for, thinking that they would see the ridiculousness of it all once they compared an inanimate object with the glory of God's visitation at the mountain. But his plan backfired. The people actually got excited about this golden calf! Didn't they know it was just a collection of all their jewelry? They couldn't be serious! In a panic, Aaron tried to sway them back to the Lord by building an altar in front of the calf and decreeing a festival in honor of the Lord, but it was too late. The people were out of control. The golden calf was their cue to indulge themselves in pagan revelry. They ate, they drank, they rose up to play and cast off their garments with wild abandon. Aaron watched and wondered how he would ever explain all of this to Moses.

He found out soon enough. Moses broke up the party with a bang. Casting down the tablets he had brought down the mountain with him, he headed straight for the golden calf with a rage in his eyes that surpassed any previous bursts of anger Aaron had witnessed in his headstrong brother. Aaron held his breath and waited for the explosion he knew would soon come his way after Moses dealt with the people. The people! It was their fault! Moses knew they were out of control when he left them in his brother's care. The spell over the entire camp broke as Moses melted down the golden calf, ground up the cooled gold, and forced the people to drink its shavings in water. Aaron, ashamed that he had allowed himself to be intimidated by the unbelieving masses, found it difficult to even confess that he had made the golden calf. So he lied, "All I did was throw the jewelry into the fire, and this calf came out. Come on, Moses. Cut me a break. Even you have trouble with these people!" But Moses only looked at him and sadly shook his head, as if confronting an incorrigible child, before turning back to the scrambling Israelites who were now being put to death in the camp.

When the furor at last subsided in the camp, Moses related to his brother what had happened on the mountain.

All of Aaron's rationale and self-justification went out the window, leaving room for true contrition in his heart. While Aaron was down below feeling alone, cut out of the picture, he had been very much on God's mind. While he was feeling ignored and underrated, God was securing his position down to the details of how he would be dressed and exactly what his job description would be. While he was feeling completely insignificant in the scheme of things, God was stressing how important Aaron would be in the order of conducting the affairs of the priesthood. Tears of repentance flowed as he realized he had been just like the people he judged. Unbelieving. Foolish and self-consumed. Aaron finally realized what Moses already knew—that the only way he could find his own worth and overcome all he had been feeling was to find himself in the presence of God.

When we have no visible proof of God
at work in our lives, it is difficult to
remember that we are very much
on His mind, still very much a part
of His active agenda.

What areas of your life do you feel God is moving too slowly in? Sad to say, many of us are guilty of feeling forgotten by God at the exact same time He sits in heaven rubbing His hands in glee over a blessing that He's busy preparing for us. When we have no visible proof of God at work in our lives, it is difficult to remember that we are very much on His mind, still very much a part of His active agenda. We forget that we are called to walk by faith and not by sight. We begin to yield to the arm of flesh. We become irritable and defensive when questioned about our actions. "Well, God didn't say anything, and I had a peace about it," we retort shortly. But where is that peace now? When we're caught in the throes of impatience, anything that drowns out the immediate longing of the flesh will give us momentary peace. Satan is always happy to hand us grease to put on the burn, knowing it will bring brief comfort before causing further damage and pain. But the peace that passes all understanding is found in keeping your mind on the One who is always thinking of you—Jesus.

Dear Heavenly Father, far too many times I have been tempted to take matters into my own hands when I don't see You coming through according to my schedule. I succumb to pressure from the expectations of those around me and resort to trying to make things happen myself. Please forgive me for the moments of murmuring and doubt that I entertain when things aren't going the way I would like them to go. Silence my fears and my doubts with Your Word. Let the Holy Spirit bring Your promises back to my remembrance and speak peace to my soul. Increase my trust in You and help me to stand fast knowing that though I cannot see physical evidence in the times I feel forsaken, You are very much present and active in my life. In Jesus' name I pray, amen.

Risky Times

*But Joshua spared Rahab the prostitute, with her family
and all who belonged to her, because she hid the men
Joshua had sent as spies to Jericho—and she lives
among the Israelites to this day.*

JOSHUA 6:25

ahab closed the door behind the last cus-
tomer and leaned against it in utter fatigue. Her spirit was
tired. Her soul ached more than her body as she blinked
back tears of frustration. Though her home was a place of
"solace" for many a stranger and traveler, she felt isolated
and lonely. She had made a profession out of relieving
others' "needs," and yet she felt so empty. Who was there
to relieve her? She tipped up her chin as if to reinforce her
resolve that a woman's got to do what a woman's got to
do in hard times. There was no one to take care of her. It
was up to her to survive as best she could, much to the
chagrin of her family. Their disappointment in her was
apparent, and it seemed as if she had no way to redeem
herself in their eyes—or in her own, for that matter. But
she refused to be the victim. At least she wasn't out there

begging. She worked for what she had, whether or not it was considered a legitimate profession. But in moments when she let down her guard, like tonight as she leaned out her window gazing long into the night and observed the serenity of the moon and the stars, she wondered if there was really a God. And if there was, would He ever take pity on someone like her? Was it possible for Him to deliver her from her circumstances?

Her gaze shifted downward, from the perfect black canopy that seemed to be adorned with diamonds suspended and shimmering as far as she could see, to the plains where it was rumored that the Israelites lay in wait, considering when best to seize Jericho. She had heard of their God and how He fiercely fought battles on their behalf. The entire city was in a state of alarm awaiting what they speculated would be certain destruction. What did you have to do to get a God like that on your side? Rahab didn't know how long she stood there pondering her fate, daring to dream of better days, before she finally closed the shutters. Whispering a prayer to whoever cared to hear, she descended into an unusually peaceful sleep.

Upon waking Rahab thought for a fleeting moment about how well she had slept—the best sleep in as long as she could remember, in fact. Usually the night was filled with troubling dreams of someone chasing her, dragging her somewhere she didn't want to go. Often she would awake drenched in sweat, trembling like a leaf. But this morning was different; she was actually refreshed. The people in the market eyed her strangely as she hummed to herself while making her rounds, gathering provisions for the day. *What is with Rahab?* she imagined them wondering. She usually sauntered through with her head held high, her face set in an emotionless mask that seemed to dare anyone to look at her in a judgmental fashion. But today, well, Rahab actually smiled!

The rest of the day passed no differently than any other, and eventually gave way to dusk. The same familiar knock came at the door, but totally unfamiliar faces stood before her when Rahab opened it. She could tell from their countenances that they were foreign; she knew by instinct that they were Israelites. Closing the door quickly behind her, she asked them to state their business, noting that they did not look like the type who were in search of her services. As they explained themselves, she knew intuitively that she must help them. Perhaps this was her last chance to escape this life if truly the city was doomed. Maybe their God would give her a chance. It was worth the risk. She could become no more an outcast than she was already. Before Rahab had finished securing their hiding place on the roof, another knock, even more urgent than the first, came. This time the king's messengers stood before her with shifty eyes, signaling for her to behave as if she didn't recognize them. They demanded that she hand over her visitors, for they were spies who would put them all in danger. Though her heart was beating wildly, she maintained her practiced blank face that was completely unreadable, informing them that the spies had left long before the closing of the city gate. Studying her face for any hint of a lie for a suspended instant in the light of the torch they carried, they concluded she would be of no further help, and they departed.

After letting the spies down through her window, Rahab secured the scarlet cord that would be her salvation in the window as she had been instructed. Again she looked heavenward. Was He really up there? "If You are, please deliver me from this nightmare," she breathed.

Over the next several days Rahab tried to pass the time as usual, but everything had changed. She now had hope. She waited until the Israelites arrived. Somberly they came, marching soundlessly around the city gates. One day, two days, three days...the silence was deafening, the tension unbearable. The entire city waited with its breath held as day after day they marched, waiting for what, no one knew. Rahab timed her visit to her family's house at a time when she knew their nerves would be too raw from fear to waste their energy on disapproving of or resisting her invitation. She knew they would be ready to embrace any solution she offered, and she was right. Willingly they sought the refuge of her home, though most people had abandoned the houses on the wall, fearing they would be attacked first. Huddled together waiting, they drew measured breaths and strained to hear into the silence as the Israelites continued their interminable march, the trudging sound they made becoming more ominous with each step. Suddenly trumpets sounded and battle cries filled the air! Rahab could feel the walls collapsing and with them her consciousness also collapsed. Strong arms lifted her, carrying her through the rubble along with the rest of her family and setting her feet on a solid rock some distance away from the chaos. She sank to the ground, weeping, thanking a God who was more merciful than she had hoped. He had saved her and her household. She had also been redeemed in the eyes of her family. And because God blessed her while she was yet unpleasing, she, in turn, would seek to please Him all her days.

What sins do you struggle with that make you feel unworthy of God's attention? There are times in our lives when, so deep is our sin in our own eyes, we are sure that God stands far off along with the rest of those who disapprove of the things that we've done. Rejection, shame, and condemnation choke out any hope we have of forgiveness, redemption, or blessing. We are almost afraid to utter a plea for help, fearing God's certain rebuttal. Yet even the most timid voice, trembling with hope the size of a mustard seed, reaches His ears, and His response is immediate—not with wasted words but with lifesaving action, so happy is He that you called. For those of us humbled by our own state of unworthiness, He supplies abundant grace.

> *Dear Heavenly Father, my sin is too much for me to bear. I have no one to turn to but You. All others have forsaken me, and though I feel as if I am drowning in unworthiness, I pray You will hear my cry. Only You can restore me and mend my heart. I ask that You would forgive me and grant me a new beginning as I choose to follow You. Grant me Your Holy Spirit to be my guide and help me to remain steadfast. Cleanse me, fill me, teach me, and lead me in the way of life everlasting. In Jesus' name, amen.*

Deciding Times

But because my servant Caleb has a different spirit
and follows me wholeheartedly,
I will bring him into the land he went to.

NUMBERS 14:24

Caleb couldn't believe his ears. When would these people ever learn? He felt the desire to shout at the top of his lungs, "You idiots! How long will you maintain this pathetic slave mentality that you can't have more than what you already possess, for heaven's sake?" All the way back from the land they'd gone to check out, Caleb was tingling. It was hard for him to walk normally. He was literally vibrating with the desire to leap and somersault all the way home. After all they had been through, this was truly worth it. God was so awesome! What a land—it literally flowed with milk and honey! The fruit was so lush that it took two men to carry a branch of grapes! It was as if God had multiplied everything in the land to make up for their time of lack and suffering. He couldn't wait to move in. And now here were these men causing needless alarm with their negative report. So what if they'd seen giants! Hadn't God delivered them from their enemies before? What was so new about this exercise? Caleb's heart sank as the moans from the crowd grew louder. He cast a glance toward Joshua, who looked as perturbed as Caleb felt. Were they the only two who believed?

Caleb pressed forward. He didn't care what they thought; he would speak his mind. "I believe we should go up and take the land. We can do it," he stated. The others bristled at his confident words, but he would not be dissuaded. He was sick of their limited mentality. Sick of their incapability to give God the honor He was due. It was downright offensive...insulting...disrespectful how they carried on every time God instructed them to do something. Caleb had a mind to leave them right there and go into the new land without them. As far as he was concerned, they didn't deserve to go if their faith in God was so minuscule. Who needed them? He didn't want to be associated with their mindset. If he was the odd man out, that was fine with him. It was hard to believe he and these people came from the same place. They saw things so differently! At first Caleb thought something was wrong with him, but when he meditated on the goodness of God, rehearsing all he had seen Him do, everything made sense. Joshua, who had spent time with the Lord in the tabernacle, had discussed this with Caleb while they were away. It seemed a repeat of when the people drew back from having individual contact with God and instead assigned Moses to bring them messages. They missed out on understanding the fullness of who He was. And therefore they struggled to trust Him constantly.

Caleb was snatched back from this train of thought by frantic voices surrounding him. The more the people mumbled, the more grieved he became. Stoning? How could they speak of stoning them? He didn't know if it was grief or madness that caused Joshua and him to begin rending their garments. The insolence of the people in the face of what God desired to do for them was heart-breaking. He could only hope that God would accept his personal apology for their disgraceful behavior. Caleb, who had followed God wholeheartedly from the time he was a child, could not relate to this blatant lack of faith. He delighted in worshiping the Lord and beholding His glory as He led the people toward the Promised Land. He believed that nothing was impossible with God. After all, he had seen Him at work. Taking possession of what already belonged to them according to the Word of God, who could not lie, was nothing compared to what they had been through already.

As he waited for Moses to return from consulting with God, his mind raced to try to anticipate God's reaction to this episode of chaos in the camp. He found out soon enough. And what happened was more horrifying than he imagined, but nothing within him could find a reason to argue with God's verdict. The other men who had gone to spy out the land, with the exception of Joshua and himself, were killed in a plague that silenced their bad report. But the worst part of all, the part Caleb and Joshua couldn't escape, was the punishment handed down to the rest of the people. They would not enter the land of promise at all. They had chosen the fate of wandering in the desert for another forty years until all of them died with their foolish words. Their children would enter Canaan, but every man and woman who had been filled with unbelief could go no further than what he or she believed. Caleb and Joshua would be allowed to go in, but they would have to wait until the new generation—the children of this generation—went in. It was excruciating to bear the weight of the others' disobedience, but Caleb comforted himself with the knowledge that God would reward his faithfulness by keeping him so that he and his descendants could claim their inheritance.

Now, forty-five years later, much had come to pass. Moses had died, Joshua now led the people, and the campaign to claim what was theirs was well underway. Caleb was now eighty-five, yet just as strong as he was on the first day that God had spoken of giving them this territory. Caleb stood before his friend and leader, Joshua, and said with the kind of boldness that comes only when you know you're backed by God, "Give me this mountain." He had never been one to run from a battle, and was ready to claim what belonged to him. The thought of a good fight right about now was rather stimulating to him. He relished the opportunity to vanquish the Lord's enemies. With Joshua's permission, Caleb set off, a purpose in his step, feeling the exhilaration of at last being in the center of God's divine will.

Isn't it a relief to know that no matter what, God's plan for your life will be intact? As long as you're willing to follow Him wholeheartedly, He remains a faithful partner even when all others bail out. Though the unbelief and negativity of those around us can cause delays in what we're ready to embrace immediately, fortunately God remains true to His Word. He marks the spot with your name and preserves what is yours to claim until the day of fulfillment. We can find peace in what seems to be a delay by remembering that as children of God we are never victims of circumstance—only participants in a plan much greater than our finite understanding, a plan in which every detail has been painstakingly worked out in God's omniscient way that culminates in His perfect timing.

*Dear Heavenly Father, so many times I feel that my
life or my circumstances have been put on hold
because of things beyond my control. Please forgive
me for forgetting that You still reign. Help me to keep
my eyes on You, following You with all my heart,
mind, and soul, even when the masses are going in
another direction. As I meditate on Your promises,
make them come alive inside of me, that I might not
be swayed by doubt, delay, or what my eyes see, but
only by what Your voice speaks. I pray that I never
treat Your promises with contempt but rejoice in all
You say and do on my behalf. Keep me sensitive to
Your voice that I might move quickly and obediently
at Your command. I claim my blessings now
according to Your promise. In Jesus' name, amen.*

It is in the valley,
in the alone
that we find ourselves
in the best of company...
this is the place where
God fills all the empty spaces
for He has finally been
given the room to do
what He does best...

Transitional Times

And Ruth the Moabitess said to Naomi,
"Let me go to the fields and pick up the leftover grain
behind anyone in whose eyes I find favor."

RUTH 2:2

Ruth arched her back, stretching out the kinks, bringing some relief to her aching muscles. As she turned slightly from side to side to ease the tension in her waist, she saw a small cluster of male workers looking in her direction. In the center of the cluster was a distinguished older man who was studying her with great interest. She hoped she wasn't trespassing on the wrong field. Her understanding was that she was free to glean behind the workers in the field. This was the law of their God— widows and others less fortunate were free to take whatever was left behind in the harvest.

How kind this God is to be so compassionate in His provision for all people, Ruth thought to herself. This was one of the reasons why she chose to follow Naomi, her mother-in-law, back to Bethlehem from Moab. After her husband, Naomi's son, had died, there was no reason to remain in Moab. Nothing tugged at her heart strongly enough to keep her there. She had grown to love not only her husband but his entire family. She loved their quiet faith and their considerate ways. She was intrigued by their God, this God who had delivered their people from slavery and brought them to a land of promise. As they rehearsed their story over the Passover meal year after year, her mind was filled with images of the death angel passing over their ancestors' houses in Egypt. Of Pharaoh and his army being drowned in the Red Sea. Of a God who led them by fire at night and by a cloud during the day. Who rained down food for them to eat and fiercely fought their enemies. Their God was nothing like the silent idols the people worshiped in Moab. Ruth had long wondered if they really heard her petitions and if the events of her life came about more by happenstance than by design, yet they were all she'd had until she met her husband and learned differently. And then he died. His brother died. His father died. She ached for Naomi as she watched her mother-in-law's faith die with the birth of such hard circumstances. Though Ruth wasn't sure that their God, this Yahweh, would have her, she vowed to have enough faith for both of them and that she would be God's arms to Naomi until she was ready to embrace Him again.

It was hard for Ruth to believe that this God she had heard so much about would abandon His people just like that. Surely He would find a way to redeem their tragedy. She would not give up on Him, even if Naomi had. So on she went with Naomi to Jerusalem, leaving all she knew behind, ready to embrace this God if He would embrace her. She felt as free as the wind that coursed through her hair as she collected the stray barley. The sun...the fresh air...she couldn't explain it, but she had such a peace, such a sense of well-being. She enjoyed her time in the fields as much as she enjoyed her evenings spent talking with Naomi, chuckling at memories of pleasant yesterdays or learning new tidbits of information from Naomi's old friends who dropped by to catch her up on all she had missed in her absence. But now Ruth felt a strange stirring in her soul. She could still feel the eyes of that man on her as she turned back to her work. She knew that her people were enemies of Israel, which made her a woman who was vulnerable to attack. So she prayed silently to this God she had come to admire for favor and protection.

A shadow fell across Ruth's path causing her to look up. *What kind eyes he has,* she thought. Not quite knowing what to say, she waited for him to speak. Truly God had taken pity on her, for here this man was extending himself in a most generous manner, offering her water, lunch, the refuge of his fields to glean in under his care. Wait until she told Naomi! Surely this would lift her faith. That it did, and more. Naomi was quick to see this as an opportunity to replace all that Ruth had lost. Ruth wasn't sure she had that much faith, but she chose to yield in respectful obedience to Naomi. It was worth doing as she said just to see the gleam in Naomi's eyes. It had been a long time since her mother-in-law had looked forward to anything; who was Ruth to disappoint her? So off to the threshing floor she went with her heart in her hands, praying to Yahweh that this kind gentleman, Boaz, would not find her proposal presumptuous.

Ruth didn't know if it was the chill of the night air or her nervousness that made her shiver so as she lay down at his feet and waited for him to discover her. Would he be willing to be her redeemer? Or would he find her—a foreigner, an outsider, an insignificant victim of circumstance—unworthy of redeeming? And then came the surprise in the middle of the night. Yes, yes, he counted it a privilege to be her redeemer, and he was willing to do whatever he had to do in order to secure this covenant!

As she returned home bearing six measures of barley in her arms and praises to this wonderful God in her spirit, she pondered this sudden turn in her fate. And she found nothing to attribute it to but Yahweh. Naomi's faith resurfaced in leaps and bounds as Ruth related the story of how Boaz had agreed to make sure the matter would be settled. The wait was not a long one, and redeem her he did. Ruth's heart felt as if it would burst with the news. She had been bought with a price, redeemed, betrothed, made worthy, restored! She was no longer a foreigner; she had been grafted into a divine family tree. This God who had once been far away had drawn nigh and poured out His mercy on her in bountiful measure, giving credence to her faith and a home to her wandering soul. As she looked from the face of her loving husband to their newborn child in her arms, this child who would be the grandfather of King David and part of the lineage of Jesus Christ, she thought of Orpah, her sister-in-law who had turned back to Moab, and wept. She wept as she pondered the emptiness of a life lived without redemption and the gratitude she felt for how God had redeemed her own life.

Do you stuggle with feelings of unworthiness and feeling forsaken? Sometimes we are tempted to think we are further away from God than we really are. Faith feels like a foreign country. And hope is but a vague memory of a better frame of mind. We feel that the circumstances of life and its inevitable hardships are proof of His distance. Perhaps we are not so important in the scheme of things. Perhaps His time would be better spent on those more worthy of His notice, those who have an "in" with Him, those who have done exploits for His Name's sake. Yet our hearts cry out for a redeemer to relieve us of our questions and our aloneness. To make us feel wanted, cherished, like we belong. And God comes bearing much more than we ever asked or hoped for. He comes bearing gifts of restoration that affirm who we are as well as where we're going. He wraps His arms around us and weaves our days into the tapestry of His divine design, making us into something beautiful, something good, something better than before.

Dear Heavenly Father, the transitions of life sometimes take their toll on my faith, causing me to question where I really stand with You. In those times I pray that You draw near and reassure me of Your presence and Your favor. As I try to find my way through the foreign nuances of where change takes me, please be the one familiar thing that I can cling to. Grant me Your promise that You will meet me in this strange place where I don't know what to do and point the way to solid ground. Order my steps and establish me in the midst of Your divine purposes. Fulfill Your plans for me according to Your promise. In Jesus' name, amen.

Timid Times

And Kish said to Saul his son,
Take now one of the servants with thee,
and arise, go seek the asses.

1 SAMUEL 9:3 KJV

Saul stood surveying the land with furrowed brow, annoyed at this task and also at his failure to accomplish so trivial a mission. Chasing donkeys! This was not what he had been created to do. Why his father insisted that this was all that Saul was up to doing was beyond him. He heaved a heavy sigh; it was downright frustrating. From the time he was born, his father treated him as if he were too delicate for real men's work. He heard constant comments about how fair of face he was. He was taller than everyone else and therefore had been the source of ridicule among the other children—out of envy, his father said. But in his heart Saul knew that one day they would all see him in a different light. He didn't quite know how, but time would tell. Just because he was handsome did not mean he couldn't be as fierce a warrior as any other man. His father was known as a valiant man. This was his heritage. One day Saul would show them all a side of himself they hadn't anticipated.

Up one hill and down the next, with no donkey in sight. After three days, Saul grew weary of this fruitless chase and decided to turn back lest his father became concerned for his welfare. But his servant suggested that they visit Samuel the seer and enlist his help, so Saul decided to go a little further. Perhaps this seer could tell them something that would redeem this boring escapade in some way before they headed back. And if he could help them locate the wandering animals, all the better.

But who can ever anticipate a day like this day, when everything in your life is set on a track you never anticipated, and your world is never the same again? Though Saul had longed to be taken seriously, the words that Samuel said to him were astonishing. King over Israel! How could that be? He was torn between elation and fear. Amazement and understanding. Samuel had said that the power of the Lord would come upon him and he would become a different person. For this he was grateful. He would need all the help he could get. Even though he had always longed for recognition as a man of true stature, now that the moment was upon him, he couldn't really say that he felt ready for it. He had been pampered; he had led an easy life. He was spoiled. And though everyone said he was the most handsome man they had ever seen, he was still just a Benjamite. And not just a Benjamite—he was from the smallest clan of the smallest tribe in Israel. Who was going to take him seriously as king? But Samuel assured him that in seven days, all he said would be fulfilled.

Saul had to admit that he did feel different as he went on his way. As the company of prophets surrounded him, the Spirit of the Lord came upon him and he began to prophesy. The word spread quickly. No one could believe it—Saul was prophesying! What had come over him? This was a side of him they had never seen. He was always so low-key—shy, as a matter of fact. He did his best to avoid the stares of those who did a double take when they saw him. Many were moved to comment on how incredibly handsome he was, and they marveled at his height—a whole head taller than everyone else in the land! While all of this would have caused some to become haughty and self absorbed, Saul became more introverted, more self-conscious. But here he was prophesying with abandon. *Since when did he get religion?* they wondered. They had never heard him say much of anything, period. And now here he stood delivering the Word of God. Well! Would wonders never cease?

And now here came Samuel, declaring that the Lord was ready to select the king that they had requested. And who did He select but this same Saul! Now the fear of failure rose up to engulf Saul. Perhaps he had been a bit hasty in his own self-assessment. So, while everyone was looking for him, he hid himself among the baggage. Some king! Yet he was the one that was crowned. The people just didn't understand God's reasoning in this matter at all. Why would He select Saul, of all people? Yes, he looked the part outwardly, but as far as they could see he was a pretty house with no one home. While some wandered away, murmuring that they were more doomed than ever before, Saul kept silent. He would show them. He would show them all.

The new king had to admit that, though Samuel had crowned him, he felt no different. So back to tending the fields he went, until the day the Ammonites besieged Jabesh Gilead. As the people wept and mourned their fate, Saul was filled with righteous indignation. Before he gave any thought to cautioning himself, the heart of a king rose up within him like the ire of a lioness protecting her cubs. So fierce was he in his call to arms that no one doubted that the Spirit of God was indeed upon him to lead the people. In the midst of routing the enemy, it finally hit Saul—this was what he had waited for all his life! A moment like this. God had heard the silent cry of his heart that he had found so difficult to express. He felt as if his desire had been buried beneath the weight of other people's doubts and his own insecurities, and it seemed as if some divine hand had cleared away all of the garbage to give him this one shot to demonstrate what he truly held within himself. Charging across the field after the enemy, Saul felt liberated. Liberated to understand that in and of himself, he would never be anything more than a prisoner of his own fears, but with God as his source, he could accomplish anything. God had given him the victory when no one else saw his potential. This humbled him. Saul felt no need to hold a grudge against his naysayers, for the truth he now clung to with both hands was too precious to let go of. God would always be his defense. This was more than enough reason to forgive and forget. It was time to celebrate.

Do you have secret aspirations hiding in your heart? Though most people have heard the old adage that you can't judge a book by its cover, many people still do. They draw assumptions based on our appearance, and voice their conclusions without stopping to consider the damage their words may cause. And then God shows up and validates our existence by setting us apart for a purpose that no one expected us to fulfill. And though respect doesn't come immediately, it does come as God's favor goes before us to set the stage for our entrance. We find ourselves as surprised as those around us once we see all that we can accomplish through His strength and wisdom flowing through us. And the rejections of the past prepare us to be gracious hosts of the blessings now at hand.

> *Dear Heavenly Father, though I struggle with many insecurities and self-inflicted limitations, I long to be all that You created me to be. Help my faith to press past the doubtful opinions of others until I reach the place of Your endless possibilities. As I remember that it is Christ in me who accomplishes all things, help me to resist the urge to draw back in fear when You are beckoning me onward. Grant me courage. Give me strength to run the race as I choose to press toward the mark for the prize of Your high call in Christ Jesus. Enable me to apprehend that for which You have apprehended me. And may all the praise I receive be as incense before Your throne as I give it back to You. In Jesus' name, amen.*

Accounting Times

Then Nathan said to David, "You are the man!
This is what the Lord, the God of Israel, says."

2 SAMUEL 12:7

athan paced back and forth in his room, as if the brisk walking would somehow erase the Word of the Lord that was like a fire in the midst of his chest. How could he deliver such a harsh word to the king? He was just a prophet. It was one thing to be sent to deliver comforting words, or words of instruction on how to proceed in warfare against their enemies. But this message was a whole universe away from the usual message he was asked to carry to King David. This was personal. This was embarrassing and shameful. Adultery! He couldn't believe it, but then again he had to, because God never lied. Yet how could he handle this delicate matter without incurring the wrath of David and those around him? The people liked David, and with good reason. The land was at peace. The economy was good. He was a fair king. He was handsome and down-to-earth. Why, he had danced out of his clothes before the Lord while celebrating a hard-won victory! He was every man's king. Full of compassion and love for God and country.

Why David had been so foolish as to take another man's wife and then have the man killed was perplexing to Nathan. Ah, but there was the child she bore! David's child. Nathan surmised the king had to cover his tracks. But did he forget that God was watching? Did he really think that this holy God would entertain, then cover, his sin? What was David thinking? This was exactly why he should have gone to war with his people, but no, David had to stay at home. What a mess! And now he, Nathan, had been instructed to go and call him on the carpet. How would he even begin to broach the subject?

Nathan took his time, putting off his task as long as he could just in case God changed His mind and decided to deal with David privately. But now the burden had grown increasingly unbearable. Indeed, he must go. As Nathan walked toward the palace, his heart was heavy. Barely acknowledging the respectful nods he received along the way, he stayed focused on his present dilemma. His pain increased as he gazed upon David, who was always so happy to see him. "What shall I say, Lord?" he breathed the question as a silent prayer while continuing to search David's face for some sort of sign...something that reassured him that he wouldn't have to go any further, but all he saw was David's face filled with anticipation, waiting to hear what Nathan had to say. And so he began by weaving an intriguing tale about the victimization of a poor man by a man of privilege. He decided he would let David judge himself in the light of this allegory, for he was merely a messenger and not the magistrate.

David pronounced his judgment on the man in Nathan's story: repayment of property and death.

Then Nathan spoke: "The man is you."

David's heart dropped as he heard Nathan's words. The judgment he pronounced would also be his own. He too would pay fourfold for his sin. Calamity would not depart from his house. His own wives would be taken in broad daylight by someone close to him. The child would die in order to preserve the name of the Lord in the sight of His enemies and waylay their contempt. As David threw himself on the mercy of God, Nathan could only encourage him to ask for God's forgiveness; the consequences would remain.

This was the part that was hard for Nathan. He loved David. He knew that the king's heart was tender toward God. He hated to see him suffer this way. Hated the disappointment and pain it inflicted on his family and household. Hated that the country had to live under the shame of its leader's mistake. But sin is sin, no matter who commits it. The silence in the halls was deafening as Nathan made his way back down the corridor and out into the open air. He felt as if his lungs would burst. Had he been holding his breath the entire time? He went home, and he waited. He prayed for David. Prayed that God's mercy would be sufficient cause for him to endure this harsh punishment like an obedient son. Prayed that God would comfort him in a special way. "Restore what he has lost, O God. Let him know that You reward a heart that is tender toward You," Nathan prayed. He dared to hope that God would show David some tenderness in the midst of this terrible experience.

And then Nathan thanked God. Thanked God that he knew Him. Thanked God that He trusted him to bear His Word, no matter how harsh it may be at times, and never sent him alone. The Lord accompanied him with the spirit of conviction. The reward for Nathan was seeing those who chose to hear restored to wholeness. Only obedience and the tender mercies of a loving God could put the pieces back together of a life shattered by sin.

And then the news came that Bathsheba would bear another son. One whom God would love. Nathan chuckled to himself. Yes, it was just like God to graciously send him back to the palace—this time bearing good news.

What incidences have you let slide in the past that you regret never speaking up about? Being the bearer of truth when others are running for cover is not the most desirable position to have, even when we're dealing with church folks. Saved or not, the truth hurts and can bring unpredictable reactions when the bearer of the message touches on a sensitive subject. Sometimes we watch as friends and family members make terrible decisions that we know will long affect their lives, and we wrestle to decide whether we should blow the whistle or keep the peace. But God urges us to speak the truth in love and allow His spirit of conviction to do the rest. It is not our job to render judgment on the offender. We are just to deliver the message, knowing that in the face of truth God always has our backs.

> *Heavenly Father, thank You for the gift of truth, for Your truth sets us free. Help me to remember this when I need to make a stand for Your Word instead of allowing those around me to continue going astray in their sin. Keep me mindful that true love is tough love which is willing to sacrifice in order to save. Help me not to fear their reactions more than the judgment that will fall on their lives. Let the desire for righteousness always prevail over all else in*

my heart. Grant me the sensitivity to know when to speak and when to remain silent. I want to be ever sensitive to Your Spirit, and obedient to Your leading. In Jesus' name, amen.

Proving Times

*He picked up the cloak that had fallen from Elijah...
and struck the water with it. "Where now is
the LORD, the God of Elijah?" he asked.*

2 KINGS 2:13,14

rom the moment Elijah approached him in the fields, Elisha knew his life would never be the same, and he was ready. Ready to bid his family farewell. Ready to follow after God. His was a restless spirit that could not be contained in the mundane affairs of everyday life; his spirit thirsted for more. More of what God had. More power to experience the supernatural. More than what others sought. So willingly he followed Elijah, but not in pursuit of just an ordinary call. Zealously he served, gleaning all he could from Elijah's words as well as his example. Elisha stored up all that he saw and heard, waiting for his own release. He did not relish the day when Elijah would leave him. Even as he thought of it, a vast, open space expanded in his heart. He knew he would feel an emptiness without his mentor. Truly, the Lord would need to be a very present

166 ⟨⟩ *Where Are You, God?*

companion in the absence of one who had filled his life with so much.

It was a lonely life, the life of a prophet. Many did not want to receive the words he brought them. But then there were also the rewarding times when God moved supernaturally on someone's behalf, supplying a need, healing a body. A myriad of experiences made him rely on the power of God more than any amount of intellectual knowledge he could muster. Yes, he would miss Elijah. He would feel most alone. This was the conversation Elisha had with himself several days before the Lord took his mentor. Without it being said, he knew it was time. But neither of them spoke of it.

He felt jolted into reality when those from the school of the prophets asked him, "Do you know that the Lord is going to take your master today?" Elisha didn't want to breathe a word of it, thinking that his silence would cause a delay. Elijah tried to ease the moment by excusing Elisha from his presence, thinking it kinder to spare his pupil the trauma of experiencing their separation firsthand. But Elisha would not hear of leaving him, remaining a steadfast companion to the end. While the others watched them from a distance, choosing not to go the extra mile in favor of remaining where they were, Elisha pressed on. As Elijah struck the waters of the Jordan with his cloak, causing the river to part and allowing them to cross over on dry ground, Elisha marveled at the ease with which this great man of God operated in his calling. He walked in the assurance of God's presence and partnership. And he knew that this was the area in which he would be tried upon Elijah's departure.

This was an important time for Elisha. This would separate the principles of what he had learned from glaring reality. Now he would have to know and experience God for himself. With Elijah absent, would God still show Himself strong in their midst? This question beat in his heart so loudly he thought he could hear it in the air. He had to follow his teacher. He had to draw on him one last time. He needed what Elijah had to go the rest of the way alone. And so he summoned his courage when Elijah turned to ask him, "What can I do for you before I am taken from you?" Elisha immediately responded, "Let me inherit a double portion of your spirit." He hoped that Elijah would not consider this too bold a request. But the old prophet actually had a glint of admiration in his eyes when he replied that if his dear pupil saw him when he was taken from him, he could have the anointing. If this was some sort of way to test Elisha's depth of commitment and discipline, he would surely pass, so desperate was he for the fullness of God's power in his life. So keeping his gaze locked on Elijah, they continued on their way.

Suddenly a horsedrawn chariot of fire separated them, and Elijah was caught up in a whirlwind. Elisha stood down below beholding it all. He tore his clothes in respectful mourning, but inwardly he rejoiced at the way in which Elijah had been taken. It was a pronounced period at the end of the most incredible sentence one could write to testify of a life surrounded by God. With a sense of reverence Elisha picked up Elijah's cloak that had fallen amidst the awesome activity, and he returned in the direction from whence he had come. When he reached the Jordan he held his breath and hesitated for a fleeting second before striking the waters. Would the same God who had been with Elijah now be with him? He would soon find out. As the waters parted, Elisha felt a burden lift from his soul. God was his friend, too!

Do you find it easy to become spiritually intimidated when you're in the company of people who seemingly have it all together with God? Whatever our own relationship with the Heavenly Father, the sense of power emanating from those people causes us to question our own qualification to call God "friend." Our list of spiritual adventures is not as sensational as theirs, so when we really need a prayer to get through we know who to call because we know that God listens to them. But then one day they are no longer there and we have to call on Abba Father for ourself. With trembling hands we reach upward, not quite knowing what to expect. At times like this we must remember that there is only one true advocate who can sweet-talk God on our behalf. His name is Jesus. Based on our relationship with Him, and His relationship with the Father, God will move the heavens and the earth on our behalf.

> *Dear Heavenly Father, I feel as though I never pray enough, I never study Your Word enough, I don't know You as deeply as I ought to. Because of this spiritual handicap, I struggle with my faith though I long to have You show Yourself strong on my behalf. Please keep Your promise to me that as I draw closer to You, You will draw closer to me. Keep me ever aware that You do not compare Your children but meet them all individually where they live. I pray that I will not stay in the same place with You but will grow ever deeper, climb ever higher, and draw ever closer to Your throne. Allow me to see Your glory and Your manifest presence at work in my life. In Jesus' name, amen.*

Intimidating Times

*And when the servant of the man of God was risen early,
and gone forth, behold, an host compassed the city
both with horses and chariots. And his servant said
unto him, Alas, my master! how shall we do?*

2 Kings 6:15 kjv

Why isn't Elisha worried? his servant wondered.
Doesn't he know this danger is too close for comfort? This
was an entirely different situation from helping needy
widows or curing one of leprosy. They were surrounded
by a hostile army and there was no escape! No one could
come to their aid; they were hopelessly trapped. But this
news did not seem to phase Elisha in the least. He simply
knelt to pray, not for God to help them but for his own
eyes to be opened. He had to admit that he was missing
something he needed to see because from where he stood
what he saw was not good. The troops of Aram were
upon them.

Serving Elisha was always an adventure, but this was a
little too much excitement for his servant's blood. It was
one thing to be working on behalf of Israel. Then he was

assured of God's interest. But was God really concerned with their personal safety? They were only two men, and he was even more insignificant than his master. Yet the answer to his questions was quickly made clear, for God opened his eyes to see the hillside around them filled with horses and chariots of fire. He was humbled by the reality of God's divine protection.

And then his master prayed another prayer: "Lord, please make them blind." And again the Lord did as Elisha asked. *Who is this God?* the servant wondered to himself as he walked with Elisha, leading this blinded army away from their doorstep and into the hands of the king of Israel. And how could He take such a personal interest in each person, no matter how great or small? This holy God, whose glory was so awesome that it had moved some to terror, would in the same breath rise to defend His own. This revelation rang in his spirit and resounded in his heart. How could anyone serve idols made of wood and stone when this living, breathing God was alive and willing to shed compassion and covering on all who worshiped Him? Of all that he had experienced while serving Elisha, this knowledge was his most precious treasure. God was interested in him, little ol' him! Let the enemy come; God would meet them. And no weapon that the enemy forged against Him would prosper.

No matter how we feel or what we

experience, God is always present.

Quick to defend and protect His own,

He will never leave us or forsake us.

When threatened emotionally, physically, or spiritually, what is your first reaction? When we walk only by what our human eyes see, we miss a greater opportunity to witness what the spirit is able to reveal by divine insight. No matter how we feel or what we experience, God is always present. Quick to defend and protect His own, He will never leave us or forsake us. This has been a constant witness in my life when I have been assaulted by jealousy or the misunderstanding of others. As He causes our righteousness to shine forth as the noonday sun, His favor goes before us to bring us to a safe haven that is out of harm's reach or the enemy's tactics for destruction. And yes, He *is* interested in little ol' you!

Dear Heavenly Father, when fear and the threats of the enemy are all that I can see, open my eyes to see Your protection. Help me to rest in the knowledge that You are ever present, always loving, always covering me. You are my fortress and my hiding place. I rest secure within the strong tower of Your countenance. Continue to light my path with Your direction. Dispel my anxieties and build my confidence in Your promises toward me. Destroy the plan of the wicked against me; arise, O Lord, and let my enemies be scattered and all their advances against me be dissipated. Help me to remember that the battle belongs to You as I stand expecting Your salvation. Surround me with Your hedge of protection. Keep me ever in the circle of Your divine and blessed care. In Jesus' name, amen.

After wandering through the myriad
of my own efforts
listening to the voices
that utter words
that solve nothing...
bring no peace,
no greater assurance...
I come to the end
of all I know
and wait for You to speak
and this is where I find
that Your presence
speaks louder than words....

Threatening Times

*Hezekiah received the letter from the messengers
and read it. Then he went up to the temple of
the LORD and spread it out before the LORD.*

2 KINGS 19:14

s Eliakim, Shebna, and Joah stood before Hezekiah with their clothing rent, relaying what the Assyrian envoy had told them, the king felt overwhelmed. Overwhelmed and perplexed. This could not be happening. How could God allow the enemy to attack them this way after all he had done to turn the hearts of the people back to Him? He had reopened the temple, reinstated the priests and the Levites, torn down all of the high places, destroyed all of the idols, *and* reinstated the Passover celebration. As a matter of fact, they had just finished having a glorious time celebrating the Lord, raising countless offerings and sacrifices to Him. Hezekiah had even gotten the people to bring provisions for the priests. All of this should have pleased the Lord greatly. But instead of the peace he'd counted on, here were his officers telling him that not only was King Sennacherib of Assyria threatening to besiege Jerusalem, but that the Lord had told him to do so! How could this be happening?

What about all of Hezekiah's religious reforms? What about the fact that he was trying to do everything right and pleasing to the Lord? Wasn't that worth anything in the sight of God? Why should the enemy attack them so fiercely when they were walking in obedience? Covered in sackcloth, he made his way to the temple of the Lord. Where else could he go in a moment like this? He made the temple his refuge and prayed, awaiting word to return to him from the officers he had sent to Isaiah. Perhaps God would arise to defend His Own Name, which Sennacherib had ridiculed, if nothing else.

And then release from fear and doubt came in the form of a message from Isaiah that bore a promise. God would indeed rise to their defense. The Assyrian king would hear a rumor, forcing him to return to his own country. But just as Hezekiah was about to breathe a sigh of relief upon receiving the report that Sennacherib would be returning home, he also received a letter from his enemy. The letter advised Hezekiah not to allow his God to deceive him into thinking he had escaped destruction. Sennacherib would be back.

These words were like a fist in Hezekiah's gut that knocked his newfound faith out of him like a gust of air. Grasping the letter and heading back to the temple, he made one more urgent plea to the only One he hoped to depend on. Prayed he could depend on. Fought with knowing he could depend on. He took the crumbled letter and placed it before the Lord. "Here, Lord, You read it. It's all there. Look at what he said about You, Lord. How can I defend what I believe about You if You don't show up? You know and I know that the Assyrians are fierce. They've laid waste to nations. God, You've got to do something. Forget about me. It is *Your reputation* that is at stake. Please God, I'm calling upon You. Deliver us so that all kingdoms on earth may know that You alone are God."

God was faithful to answer. "I heard you, Hezekiah. There's nothing to worry about. What Sennacherib doesn't know is that he only won all those other victories because I ordained it so. But now, because he has chosen to disrespect Me, I am ordaining his defeat. I will give you a sign of My provision to My people, and tonight I will pay Sennacherib a little visit."

As Hezekiah rested in what the Lord had told him, the angel of the Lord put to death one hundred and eighty-five men in the Assyrian camp. When the rest arose in the morning to find themselves surrounded by corpses, they fled along with their king back to Nineveh. And as this same king who reviled the name of the Lord bowed to worship his own god, Nisroch, his own sons murdered him. And all of Israel learned that the threatenings of the enemy are no match for the favor of God.

What happens to your faith when the enemy threatens? Just about the time we experience a mighty move of God in our life or some incredible spiritual breakthrough, Satan attacks. He hits hard and leaves us reeling. *What just happened?* we wonder. *If God's really who He says He is, then why is this happening?* It is important to remember that at a time like this, God has not moved off His mark. He is still very much in the same spot where we found Him. But with every spiritual advance, we must be ready for retaliation on the part of the enemy of our souls. This is merely spiritual warfare. Warfare we've been equipped to handle. And when we can't deal with it anymore, we get out of the way and give God center field. He is always fit for the battle.

> *Dear Heavenly Father, I struggle so often with the question that if You love me, why do You allow the enemy to threaten and abuse me so? And even though I know that all things work for the ultimate good of the kingdom, as I learn how to persevere and possess my soul in patience, I am still tempted to feel momentarily forsaken. And then You reveal Your presence, and I am ashamed of my doubts. I think of what an insult it must be to You that I don't trust You more. So I repent of my ways. But my desire is this—I would like to get to the place where I don't race through the whole gamut of emotions before running back to You. Please teach me how to stead-fastly trust You in spite of what I hear, see, or experience, that I may serve You more effectively and perfect my witness to those around me. In Jesus' name, amen.*

Rebuilding Times

I went to Jerusalem, and after staying there three days I set out during the night with a few men. I had not told anyone what my God had put in my heart to do for Jerusalem. There were no mounts with me except the one I was riding on.

NEHEMIAH 2:11,12

Scanning the rubble, Nehemiah shook his head in dismay. Was he the only one who felt an overwhelming sense of pain looking at the wall in such a state of wreckage? Was this his burden and his burden alone? Had no one who had been living in Jerusalem been a little upset by this sight? He could no longer dwell on this; he only knew of one way to get rid of a burden, and that was to do something about it. If the desire to rebuild the wall was truly a nudge from God, He was well able to make provision for the task. This He had already proven. The king of Persia had been most generous to release Nehemiah from his post of serving him in order to let him begin this project. He had even contributed timber for the gates to the city and a cavalry to escort Nehemiah back in safety. This was much to the chagrin of the Israelites' enemies.

Yes, Nehemiah had come this far knowing that even to be standing in the midst of the wreckage was a miracle. He had been one of the exiles in Persia. He had felt the loneliness of being a stranger in a foreign land. Of struggling to deal with different languages, a different culture, even different gods. This is where he had felt most isolated. He clung to Yahweh with a fervency that many others hadn't managed to maintain. Thus, their captivity was the consequence. Yet God had remained faithful to Nehemiah throughout his stay, for God had crowned him with favor even in the midst of his captivity. And Nehemiah, for his part, had never let go of God's hand. He walked with Him. He talked with Him. He counseled with Him on every decision, every step of the way. And God was always there with the answer. As cupbearer to the king, Nehemiah was highly trusted—again, the providential hand of God at work. So when the exodus of the exiles back to Jerusalem began, Nehemiah, knowing he had not been put in such a prized position for nothing, stayed behind to wait on the voice of God for direction.

A visit from Nehemiah's brother bearing news of home was bittersweet. The joy of seeing his sibling was overshadowed by his report that those who survived the exile were back in the province deeply troubled and disgraced. The wall of Jerusalem had been broken down and its gates burned with fire. This so grieved the heart of Nehemiah that all he could do was weep. This was beyond distressing. How could he bear the weight of it? Then again, he was but one man. Those who had returned had not received the burden to do anything about this situation, yet he felt his heart would burst if things were not made right. He set his face to fast and pray before God, putting Him in remembrance of His word concerning the care of His people. He, Nehemiah, was willing to do his part to repair the broken places. But he couldn't do it alone. If God would be his ally, he would go.

The next day, King Artaxerxes noticed the forlorn countenance of Nehemiah and inquired about it. Once again Nehemiah breathed a prayer to God, asking for the right words to say. He then voiced his concern about the condition of his homeland, and the king asked Nehemiah his desire. This was his cue. "All right, Lord, here we go." He asked for the king's permission to go and rebuild the wall. His prayer was answered when the king consented. In the midst of opposition without and within, Nehemiah began a great work and refused to come down until it was finished. Unwavering in the face of threats, apathy, fearfulness, corruption, greed, and selfishness, Nehemiah refused to listen to any voice other than God's, and that one voice led him to the place of victory. It was a good work, and a good work always commands that God be glorified. And so it was that even their enemies were forced to accept the fact that this nation was not forsaken by its God. For only by the help of God had this work been completed.

A cause burns in our soul, and we ask ourself, "Doesn't anyone else see this great need as glaringly as I see it?" And then we find that God has allowed this vexation to spur us to rise to the occasion because, from the beginning, this was our God-ordained task. "But I feel ill-equipped to tackle this situation!" we think to ourselves. And God answers, "In and of yourself you are, but with My help nothing will be impossible to you." As we put our hand in His, He goes before us with His favor and provision. The Holy Spirit brings up the rear, saying, "This is the way; walk ye in it." And Jesus continues to intercede on our behalf and grant us the authority to step out in faith. Gazing in amazement at the accomplishment of what seemed to be an insurmountable task, we pause to give thanks, only long enough to receive the next phase of God's vision…but by this time we're ready.

Dear Heavenly Father, in my quest to find my purpose, I am overwhelmed at how limited I am in my own humanness. I long to do so much, and yet I feel so ill-equipped. And You come to me lovingly, reminding me that in my weakness Your strength is perfected in me. That You surpass my limitations in Your omniscience. And so I hold out my hands and yield them to You, right now. Holy Spirit, I yield to Your direction. Jesus, I rely on the strength of Your blood and Your authority to complete the work You've put before me. Help me to rest in the knowledge that what You commission, You also make provision for. In Jesus' name, amen.

Steadfast Times

*All the royal officials at the king's gate knelt down
and paid honor to Haman, for the king
had commanded this concerning him.
But Mordecai would not kneel down or pay him honor.*

ESTHER 3:2

The waves of contrition that swept over Mordecai were overwhelming. Covered in sackcloth and ashes, he wove his way through the streets. It seemed as if the city had literally screeched to a halt, as other Jews filled the streets weeping and wailing. One would have thought that some beloved leader had been prematurely cut down in the prime of his life. But instead it was their own fate that provoked this state of distress. And no one felt the burden of despair more than Mordecai, waves of condemnation engulfing him as he blindly staggered toward the palace gate. He felt as if it was all his fault. Had his refusal to compromise truly been an issue of standards, or had it been the fruit of his own pride? Whatever the answer to this question, it no longer mattered. His unwise actions had signed a death warrant for his people. He felt like David, crying, "May those who hope in You not be disgraced because of me, O Lord, the Lord Almighty: may those who seek You not be put to shame because of me."

Mordecai's thoughts now flitted to Haman, who had concocted this insidious scheme. How was it possible for anyone to be that evil? What a coward! The war was between the two of them. No one in his right mind could possibly be that vindictive. And yet vindictive is exactly what Haman had been, going as far as offering to pay ten thousand talents of silver into the royal treasury to fund the annihilation of the Jews. All because Mordecai refused to bow before him in the gates! When the king's officials had questioned his attitude, he had simply replied that he was a Jew. Everyone knew that a Jew would only bow to Yahweh. No one else would be acknowledged as God beside Him or before Him. For Haman to take this personally—and to this extent of retribution—was reprehensible.

And yet Mordecai had an even deeper question burning in his inner man. Where was God in all of this? How could He have let this happen? To be exiled to this place had been bad enough. The prophets had told them to do business, build homes, and be given in marriage in this place because they would be there for seventy years. And so the people had done just that. After they were free to return to Israel, many had remained to enjoy the fruit of their labor. They had done well for themselves in the midst of exile. And now this second wave of senseless cruelty! It was all Mordecai's fault. Well, if it was all his fault and God continued to be silent, then he would have to redeem himself by finding a solution. Esther, his niece—the queen—must know of this immediately.

But Esther sent a message back, saying that no one could approach the king without being summoned. This simplistic response was not cause for pause as far as

Mordecai was concerned. What difference did it make at such a time as this? It was a matter of choosing which way you wanted to die—losing your life attempting to save your people or being cut down in the free-for-all that had been sanctioned by the king. If Esther didn't get his attention, did she really think she would escape from behind the walls of her ivory tower? No, indeed, for the edict would render her a victim as well. For she also was a Jew. Perhaps this convicting message had jolted her out of her state of denial. She had called for a three-day fast, and then she would go before the king, come what may.

Three days came and went, and still Esther sent no word. As Haman passed him on his way home from a special banquet Esther had prepared for him and the king, their eyes met briefly—Mordecai's blank and unemotional, Haman's practically glowing with intense hatred. His parting glare promised vengeance. *What was his niece doing entertaining the enemy?* Mordecai wondered. This was not how he would choose to take action, but he would be patient and give her the benefit of the doubt. Esther had always been a smart girl. Perhaps now she would see that God's blessings do not come without a price. As Mordecai made his way home later that evening he noticed that Haman was having gallows built—for his neck, he presumed.

The next morning brought even stranger events, yet even so, Mordecai began to understand the mind of God a little more. He couldn't quite see where God was headed in this matter, but He certainly had a sense of humor, Mordecai wryly conceded. The royal officials had arrived bright and early, tersely ordering him to follow them. And there stood Haman with a look of hatred so intense that Mordecai wondered if his eyeballs would pop right out of his head at any given moment. As Mordecai resigned himself to being the first one killed at the hands of his enemy, the tables turned in a most unexpected twist of events. Mordecai was hoisted atop one of the royal horses, draped in a royal robe, and led through the city streets by Haman, who proclaimed, "This is what is done for the man the king delights to honor!"

It seemed that in the middle of the night, the king had a bout of insomnia and called for the annals of his kingdom to be read. As the highlights were reviewed, it was noted that Mordecai had once uncovered a plot against the king's life and had never been rewarded. Haman had hastened to the king's chambers early that morning to solidify his permission to hang Mordecai on the gallows he had built. He arrived just in time to suggest an extravagant reward for someone who had pleased the king—the rewardee remaining nameless—and was ordered to deliver the king's reward. A tiny smile played at the corner of Mordecai's lips. *Yes, God moves in mysterious ways,* he thought. And he had a feeling that he was just getting a glimpse of the beginning.

***Just when you think God has left you
at the mercy of others, "Vengeance is
mine," sayeth the Lord.***

Have you experienced a time in your life when someone came against you? King David said it best: "He prepares a table before me in the presence of my enemies." This seems inconceivable until you've lived it. I remember years ago when I was working at an ad agency under a superior who decided from the day he entered the company that he would be my ruination. He set his face against me with such a vengeance it was alarming. I struggled between my reaction to his vendetta and what I knew the Word of God advised me to do. I simply could not pray for this person. I wanted him to be struck by lightning! But then one night I broke through. With the help of the Holy Spirit, I prayed for my enemy until I felt a sense of peace settle over me. Three days later he was fired. The last I heard of him, his wife had left him and he was driving a taxicab. He had lost everything he prided himself on—position, power, prestige. I found myself reaching out to him in compassion. Amazing! Just when you think God has left you at the mercy of others, "Vengeance is mine," sayeth the Lord.

> *Dear Heavenly Father, in the midst of the enemy's attack, I often forget that You are my greatest defense. You are my rock, my fortress, my strong tower! How good it is to know that You are my Abba Father, my Protector! I can run into Your arms and trust You to rise up against those who set their faces against me. Help me to constantly seek Your peace and let You fight my battles as only You can. Also search my heart that no open door may be found. Give me a clean heart, and renew a right spirit within me that I might always bear fruit that will glorify You as I stand in the midst of the fray. In Jesus' name, amen.*

Intolerant Times

When Esther's words were reported to Mordecai,
he sent back this answer:"Do not think that because you are
in the king's house you alone of all the Jews will escape."

ESTHER 4:12

rinking in deep gulps of air, Esther disciplined herself to breathe deeply. *Well, here goes,* she thought. Even as she approached the king's court, she felt as if she were in the midst of a dream. She was the queen. She was not supposed to be fearing for her life. It was so ironic. There was no running away from who you really were, no matter how high you had risen. Her Uncle Mordecai had certainly reminded her of that. She was the envy of all her friends who had known her as a child. She had been chosen by the king to be queen of the most powerful nation in the world. Not bad for a little Jewish girl from the wrong side of the tracks. She had made it. At this point in time that almost seemed laughable, so ironic were the circumstances. Underneath all the outward finery Esther was still who she was, the product of those who had been exiled to a strange land—tolerated, but certainly not embraced or exalted. No amount of perfume or costly jewelry could erase her true heritage. Her past had come back to haunt her. The lives of the Jews were once again being threatened and, though she was queen, she was among the endangered. The king would know soon enough what she had not revealed all this time. Would his love for her turn to hatred? Would he be repulsed once he uncovered her true identity? Esther did not know quite what to expect as she drew closer to her destination. *My life is ultimately in God's hands,* she surrendered. *Let Him do with it what He may.*

And so she went, unconsciously smoothing her royal robes with her hands, not realizing that the intensity of her emotions brought a flush to her cheeks and a brilliance to her eyes that was breathtaking to all who witnessed her passage. She felt strangely calm as she entered the inner court to stand in the king's hall. So focused was she on the direness of the situation that she was thrown off-balance by the king's enthusiastic greeting. Touching the cool tip of his scepter, she was lifted out of her state of astonishment as she realized that king had no idea how his decree to annihilate the Jews had affected her. She would proceed with caution as she awaited the right time to broach the subject. Perhaps God would give her some sign, some word. For up to the present, He had been strangely silent.

Up to half the kingdom was a flattering offer in exchange for the pleasure her visit brought to him. He was a strange man, her husband. His former queen had refused his invitation to come and therefore had been banished from the kingdom while she, Esther, came unbidden, breaking the rules, and was offered up to half the kingdom! She would mull over this later, but for now the immediate issue was at hand. Though complimentary, half the kingdom would not solve her present pressing dilemma. She needed the lives of herself and her people thoughout the entire kingdom to be saved. Perhaps a dinner invitation for the king and Haman, the culprit of this whole dastardly design, would stave off this matter for a little while longer.

Was it the favor of God or the king's love for her that caused him to be so gracious this night, again offering her half the kingdom after supper? But still Esther felt no release in her spirit to state her request. Perhaps she would invite him to dinner again. He seemed so pleased that she, unlike everyone else who surrounded him, asked for nothing except the privilege of serving him. This simple gesture helped spur his generosity. And though his vile companion Haman made her stomach turn every time she looked at him, she would buy time with this second invitation. She asked for God to give her wisdom.

Halfway through this second dinner Esther was still waiting for God to give her direction, but she heard nothing, felt no inkling. Then the king was saying it again, "I will give you up to half the kingdom. Give me your request." And she heard God in the midst, telling her something glaringly obvious: "If he is willing to give you up to half the kingdom, wouldn't he grant you your life?" Of course! She had offered him everything she had but the truth. Her need. And so she stood before the king asking simply for him to redeem her and her people from the slaughter his friend Haman had orchestrated. The king, outraged that anyone would seek to harm the object of his affection, was compelled to take a walk and assess this matter from a calmer perspective. Haman, as the guilty usually do, unwisely stayed behind to beg for Esther's mercy. Falling on her couch in desperation, he further inflamed the ire of the king, who immediately sentenced him to death and gave his estate to Esther.

But this was a small comfort to her. And she pleaded with her husband, "If it pleases the king, and if he regards me with favor and thinks it the right thing to do, and if he is pleased with me, let an order be written overruling this edict. For how can I bear to see disaster fall on my people? How can I bear to see the destruction of my family?" My people, my family! It was no longer a secret. It didn't matter who she was. The king loved her. He would honor her request based on that love. And this was where God had been manifesting Himself soundlessly. For love made identity, and all the prejudices of people, a non-issue. Love exposed all secrets without judgment. But most wonderful of all, love covered the past and secured the future.

What issues about yourself constantly rise to haunt you? Sad to say that for many, no matter how successful they are, they still suffer from the prejudice of others or their own self-loathing based on outward appearance, ethnicity, or culture. No amount of power, success, or acquisitions can numb the sting of a judgment made in ignorance or a slight made consciously. But God is still present, giving grace to the humble, extending the offer of the kingdom to those who will come to Him. As we dwell in the midst of rightstanding with Him, He grants us His peace and a joy that cannot be stolen. Our rest is complete when we realize that as long as He regards us with favor because we please Him and serve Him, He will think it only right to rise up and deal with our enemies.

> *Dear Heavenly Father, You and You alone are my*
> *Lord and King. You alone can be my rescuer. Help*
> *me to rest in Your arms when my own fears and the*
> *intimidation of others come against me. As the*

threats of the enemy attempt to penetrate my psyche and I rationalize that I don't deserve Your consideration based on my shortcomings, I appeal to Your mercy and Your favor. Not on the basis of who I am or what I've done, but simply on the merit of Your love for me and the fact that I am Your child. Surround me with Your care and keep me within the realm of Your constant protection. In Jesus' name, amen.

Unexplainable Times

What strength do I have, that I should still hope?
What prospects, that I should be patient?

JOB 6:11

$\mathcal{S}$itting among the ashes with sackcloth draped gingerly over his shoulders, Job recounted the events gone by. Trying to find rhyme or reason for why his life had gone so strangely awry, he searched in vain and found no explanation for the unexplainable series of events that had totally devastated his world. He squeezed his eyes shut to stave off the waves of nausea that assailed him from the smell of the open sores that now covered his body from the top of his head to the bottom of his feet. But shutting his eyes only brought back memories of events more painful than his current discomfort.

His trusted servant, more distraught than out of breath, had informed him that the Sabeans had carried off all of his oxen and donkeys and killed all of his servants. Before Job could stop to digest this news, another servant came running from the opposite direction, crying and clutching his chest in despair. He reported that the Chaldeans had formed three raiding parties that swept down upon Job's land, carrying his camels away and killing all of his servants. As Job staggered to take in all of this information and compose himself, yet another servant arrived bearing the most devastating news of all. While attending a feast at their oldest brother's house, all of Job's children had died as a mighty wind swept in from the desert and flattened the house where they were eating.

Though overwhelmed by grief and a sense of great loss, it never entered Job's heart to lay any of his misfortune to God's charge. He remained steadfast in his faith, concluding that it was God's right to take away as well as to give. And as he bowed to worship, he laid his aching heart upon the altar, praying that in the midst of his submission he would find out why all of this had occurred. It was the most he could hope for. For the truth of the matter was that he'd had a good life which he could not claim sole responsibility for. God had been gracious, giving him much when he had entered the world empty-handed. Why should he expect to leave with anything more? With this thought he comforted himself and waited for God to explain.

But as we know, life is never fair. Just when you think things can't get any worse, they do. Even Satan knows that the effect of tragedy from without brings an altogether different reaction than when trouble strikes from within. As his body was racked with pain and disease, his wife bitterly uttered the unthinkable: "Why don't you just curse God and die?" Job cringed at the sting of her words. How could the person who was closest to him assault his faith at a time like this? His faith was all he had left. He refused to be swayed from that which he held fast. God had to still be there somewhere, working something out on his behalf. His mind struggled to search his heart for any evidence of foul play toward God, yet he found none. He was sure he had crossed all his *t*'s, dotted all of his *i*'s. He had even offered up sacrifices to the Lord just in case he or his family had done anything wrong. Yes, he was at a loss...yet the trouble had to be brought on by him. It couldn't be God, could it?

Such was the state Job's friends found him in. Sitting silently and waiting for him to speak, they were the total picture of commiseration. That is, until Job broke the silence by ruing the day he was born. On that note they felt at liberty to begin their own evaluation of Job's plight, which seemed to bear a slight resemblance to things that he had said. Job found this all quite ironic. Here he sat, a man who had been one of the richest in the region and renowned for his wisdom. He had counseled many, unfolding the mysteries of God to them as best he knew how. He had been respected and revered as a man who knew God and was highly favored by Him. Yet here he sat, submitting himself to the advice of friends who, though they meant no harm, were adding insult to injury by throwing his own theories back in his face.

How could they say that Job had some secret sin and simply needed to come clean? As God was his witness, he had done nothing wrong. Next they would be accusing him of not having enough faith! And that would be the last straw. Their company had first brought Job a slight degree of comfort, but the solace they now offered him in the form of misplaced advice only heightened his distress. He was most alone in his dilemma. He was incapable of comforting himself. He did not understand what had happened, why God had allowed these things to afflict him. No one understood. No one had the answers—not him, not his wife, not his friends. Not even the bystander who finally added in his five cents' worth, stating that it was

Job's pride which had gotten him in trouble. No, not even the bystander knew. Only God knew. And yet He did not speak. What was He waiting for? Did He even care what they thought? Truly, Job had come to the end of himself and there was nowhere else for him to go.

And then God came on the scene, His voice breaking through all of their perceptions and rationalizations like a fresh September wind. Who did any of them think they were? Before they were, He was, and would be forevermore. His counsel was greater than the greatest schemes of men, His designs more intricate than anything they created. He had never left or forsaken Job; He had merely chosen to reveal another side of Himself to him—the side that could not be contained in men's conclusions, the side that was greater than the box of rituals, formalities, and isms that Job had rehearsed and could now do by rote. Yes, He was much bigger than all of that. After all was said and done, when one understood nothing, one single fact should shine out of the darkness—God is sovereign. God is Father. God is always present. And with that He extended His grace to Job as He urged him to pray for his friends and restored to him all that he had lost, and more.

Perhaps in times when we don't feel
God beside us, He has simply left
room for us to grow.

When was the last time your faith was tested? It is the stretching past what we know that hurts most. And yet we are called to learn line upon line, precept upon precept. To go from glory to glory in our Christian experience. Yet we often wonder, *Why do bad things happen to good people?* We have no rational explanation, yet beautiful pictures of God's love and caring surround us constantly. Consider the love on a father's face as he watches his toddler attempting to walk. His desire for his child to grow to the next level causes him to stand just out of reach. Close enough lest the toddler begin to fall, but far enough to inspire the object of his affection to move toward him. Perhaps in times when we don't feel God beside us, He has simply left room for us to grow by reaching past where we've always been to a higher place, drawing us closer to Him.

> *Dear Heavenly Father, when troubles come, help me not to ask why but to have an expectancy of Your purpose being revealed. Let my mind be kept in perfect peace as I keep my eyes on You, awaiting Your direction for the way that I should take. Help me not to resist the growth but to embrace the times of pruning, that I might be more fruitful. Remind me that life is a journey and that You are present every step of the way, even when trouble cuts off my vision of You. As I cling to Your promise that all will work to the good because You love me and I am called according to Your purpose, speak comfort to my heart and wisdom to my mind, that I might stand unwavering, no matter how great the test. And no matter what the masses—those both caring and uncaring—are saying, help me keep my ears open to Your voice only. In Jesus' name, amen.*

Reproving Times

At that time the Lord spoke through Isaiah son of Amoz.
He said to him, "Take off the sackcloth from your body
and the sandals from your feet." And he did so,
going around stripped and barefoot.

ISAIAH 20:2

saiah took a deep breath and started walking. Soon the silence around him was deafening as people stared in unbelief at the naked prophet gingerly making his way through the streets. As his bare feet grew accustomed to the heat of the ground that had been baked in the noonday sun, his posture grew more upright, his steps more purposeful. As he passed bystanders, the hum began. What was Isaiah trying to prove with this outrageous illustration? They had grown used to his warnings of God's punishment, but this took the cake! Now not only was it uncomfortable for everyone who was witnessing this sight, it was downright embarrassing. Did the prophet have no shame? If he didn't think enough of himself to end this foolish charade, then he should at least think of his family. What of his sons and his wife, a prophetess in her own right? How must they feel about this? Surely God would never tell him to do something this outrageous. Perhaps Isaiah had finally gone mad from all of his ramblings. Honestly, all this talk of judgment must have truly gone to his head and pushed him over the edge!

Inwardly, Isaiah moaned with deep pain over the stubbornness of these people who refused to see or hear what God was trying to tell them. When would they stop leaning on the arm of flesh and lean instead on the One who never failed to prove that He alone was able to keep them as a nation? If only they could see God as Isaiah had seen Him, high and lifted up with His train filling the temple. His glory was indescribable in mortal language. As heavenly creatures filled the air with praises to God, Isaiah had been overcome with a deep sense of his own unworthiness. The holiness of God was so clearly evident, so pronounced that it permeated everything around him. How could he cry "holy" and sing praises to God when his own lips were so unclean? God's awesomeness and majesty was such a sharp contrast to Isaiah's own filthiness that he felt more naked in the presence of God clothed than he did walking down the street disrobed with every human eye upon him. And then the Lord had asked for someone who would go to the people for Him and Isaiah had volunteered, perhaps not realizing the depth of the assignment, but never regretting the day he said "yes" to the Lord.

Though this was a far cry from the aristocratic life Isaiah had been born into, he wouldn't trade a day of it to walk in spiritual mediocrity. So as the people passed around him, scoffing at the warnings he brought forth, he continued his naked illustration for the next three years. It was not an easy life, and it was dangerous for a prophet like Isaiah. Some of his prophecies would not come to pass for a hundred years or more; therefore, he risked being called a false prophet and being stoned. But he continued to speak what God put on his heart with such boldness that, though most attempted to ignore it, the people could never quite shake the unsettling feeling that washed over them after hearing his words. His words had a ring of truth to them, whether they wanted to hear it or not.

God had warned Isaiah that the people wouldn't listen, but He told him to speak anyway for the sake of those who eventually would listen. So, swimming against the tide of resistance, insults, fickle allegiances, and outright provocation, Isaiah delivered the startling forecast of things to come. It was with a made-up mind and a settled heart that he walked the streets alone, looking for no reward, accolades, or even a sense of understanding from those around him. Though naked, he held his head aloft, considering it a privilege to release all that he was into the arms of his God. And in that there was no shame.

What hard thing has God asked of you? Working in the Lord's service calls for a life that holds nothing back for itself. The things God asks of us can be unnerving if we have not yet purposed to be completely sold out to Him. In a world where so many carefully construct impenetrable facades, He demands from us a willingness to be open, vulnerable, and transparent. He calls us to return back to our original state of being naked and unashamed. He longs to be our only covering. The tidy lives that we have constructed to win the approval of man are nothing more than poorly made papier-mâché masks, shattered completely at the first blow of a crisis. But the faithfulness of God is always secure, covering us in righteousness, shutting out the coldness of uncertainty about the future. In Him our today, tomorrow, and eternity are securely wrapped.

> *Dear Heavenly Father, I open my heart and all that I am to be totally open and transparent before You. As I strip myself of all that is displeasing to You, cover me with Your righteousness. Let me not be ashamed in the midst of the people or feel pressured by my peers to walk contrary to Your Word. Help me to rise above popular opinion and set myself apart to be obedient to Your Word. Grant me a vision of who You are. Let me see Your holiness. As I repent, cleanse my lips. Give me a clean heart and a spirit that seeks to serve You above all else. Take my gift of service and use it to the utmost that by all means some will be saved, to the furtherance of Your kingdom. In Jesus' name, amen.*

Between the noise and the silence
a gentle breeze blows...
between my shouting fears
and mute questions
peace stands awaiting my
acknowledgment.
Never insistent,
always patient,
watching,
waiting for me to notice
that this is where I always find
the One that I am seeking
at the end of myself
and all I know...

Opposing Times

*But Daniel resolved not to defile himself with
the royal food and wine, and he asked the chief official
for permission not to defile himself this way.*

DANIEL 1:8

While the others oohed and aaahed at the splendor
of their surroundings, Daniel soundlessly took it all in.
Yes, it was lovely, but then again so was the temple in
Jerusalem before these same people—these people who
paid tribute to their ability to produce such grandeur—had
ransacked it. No, he was not moved by what he saw. He
was only moved by the glory of God. Only He deserved
such praise. And so Daniel sat, an old man in a young
boy's body, somberly watching all the pomp and circumstance swirling around him. As platters of food were set
before them along with all sorts of liquid libation, Daniel
decided to himself that the others could do what they
liked; he would not eat their food. He would not allow
their delicacies to dull his senses. He wanted to be ever
aware of all that transpired around him, for who knew

when deliverance might come? Whenever it came, he would be the first to be ready. In the meantime, he would make a stand for the God of his fathers whether the people liked it or not.

His decision proved to be a wise one, much to the surprise of the attending eunuchs. His appearance, along with that of his friends, Shadrach, Meshach, and Abednego, was far healthier than those around them who ate whatever gastronomical feast was set before them. And God caused Daniel to excel in all wisdom and understanding, even giving him dreams and visions along with their interpretations. All marveled at his wisdom and his constant elevation in the king's service. Though in the midst of enemy territory, Daniel triumphed and was given authority. As he continued to walk in favor, gaining the trust of the king, others around him were incensed by what they misinterpreted as human favoritism.

Through three administrations Daniel continued to walk an uncompromising life in the midst of Babylonian society. He was in Babylon, but clearly not of it. Though renamed Belteshazzar, he continued to answer to Daniel. He was not moved by what moved others; his mind was set on a greater kingdom, on a greater King. Others knew it, and they used this knowledge to set him up for destruction. After searching but not finding dirt on Daniel that would set the king against him, they appealed to the king's ego to challenge Daniel's faith. No man was to pray to any god or man except the king for the next thirty days. Yet Daniel continued to pray to his God. When they caught him, he was on his knees seeking his God. So they threw him into the lions' den and left him there to die. But Daniel trusted God in the dim of the cave. Though he at first could see nothing, could sense nothing except the presence of the lions surrounding him, he stood fast. As his eyes adjusted, his faith grew. As his faith grew, his sight became clearer and he beheld an awesome sight. The angel of the Lord was shutting the mouths of the lions!

So troubled was the king that, while Daniel rested in confidence in the midst of lions, he found that peace had escaped him. Continuing to mutter his parting words to Daniel almost as a mantra, the king clung to them to bolster his own hopes: "O Daniel, may your God, whom you serve continually, rescue you!" He needed to see this for himself. For if someone could serve his God so diligently, surely that God would show Himself strong on his servant's behalf! He needed to see and know that there was a God beyond the inanimate gods of Babylon that never answered back despite the false reports of many who guarded their own desperate need to believe in something. The king could barely wait for the first streams of light to herald in the dawn. He hurried back to the lions' den to determine Daniel's fate. And there was Daniel, as composed as always, resting in the knowledge of His God, completely unharmed. *Had he been at all afraid?* the king wondered in amazement.

One had to conclude that if Daniel had ever been afraid, it was before he had a revelation of who his God really was. No, there was no fear in his eyes—only the glow of knowing that, even when he was surrounded by the enemy, God was with him. As Daniel watched the king of Babylon prepare to issue a decree that all nations and men of every language throughout the land must fear and reverence the God of Daniel, he came to a place of quiet acceptance. He realized that, though Babylon was not his favorite place to be, he was exactly where he should be. The trials he had experienced were all worth it if this was the fruit that they bore. His life for God's kingdom. Daniel thought it a privileged exchange.

Can you relate to Daniel? Many Christians struggle with the weariness of working a secular job. The pull to eat what the world eats is strong, and it causes many to stumble. In the end they resemble the world too closely. The struggle to master the flesh becomes too overwhelming for many, and they seek a safer environment in which to work out their salvation, so to speak. They feel that they only can live the Christian life by escaping to the mission field or some other sort of Christian work or ministry. Yet according to the Bible, those who dared to work alongside the heathen and held fast to the hand of God affected nations for Him. Yes, they felt alone. Yes, they encountered those who plotted against them because of their faith. It seems as if experiencing opposition was part of the job description, yet they persevered. These men of God, like Daniel, chose to serve God continually no matter what. And the presence and favor of God was their reward. He did not disappoint them; He glorified Himself in their midst and affected the changing of hearts around them toward the kingdom of heaven. This is why we all are here.

> *Dear Heavenly Father, forgive me for the many times I complain about my job, the people, and even the circumstances of my situation. Please help me to see these as opportunities to effect change in the lives of many for the furtherance of Your kingdom. Let my heart beat for the people around me the way Your heart does. Let me feel Your love, compassion, and concern for them. Help me not to maximize their faults and minimize their need for You. I now cast off all self-righteousness and spiritual pride and ask that You fill my heart with all I need in order to minister effectively to the people in my workplace. Help me to exercise wisdom so that my witness will be*

*effective before others. Grant me discernment and
understanding to see past the outside of those
around me and right into their hearts. Use me
according to Your will to effect change in their lives.
In Jesus' name, amen.*

Confronting Times

And Nebuchadnezzar said to them, "Is it true, Shadrach,
Meshach and Abednego, that you do not serve my gods
or worship the image of gold I have set up?...But if you
do not worship it, you will be thrown immediately
into a blazing furnace. Then what god will be able
to rescue you from my hand?"

DANIEL 3:14,15

What new brand of foolishness had the king thought up this time? Shadrach, Meshach, and Abednego looked from one to the other. There was no need to vocalize what they were thinking. They all knew without saying that this newest project of Nebuchadnezzar's was intolerable in the eyes of the God they served. They could not—and would not—participate in his latest mad escapade. Let the chips fall where they may. As far as they were concerned, the positions they held were the handiwork of God, not the product of some gracious Babylonian who thought himself more important than he ought. So let them blow the trumpets and play their musical instruments; they would not bow down to any golden images of anything!

They had already anticipated the king's outrage when he received the news of their obstinance, and they made up their minds that if they had to die for what they believed, so be it. And so they stood, staunch and erect, not flinching even in the face of Nebuchadnezzar's displeasure. His threats inspired no fear in them, and their answer to him was simple and direct: "O Nebuchadnezzar, we do not need to defend ourselves before you in this matter. If we are thrown into the blazing furnace, the God we serve is able to save us from it, and He will rescue us from your hand, O king. But even if He does not, we want you to know, O king, that we will not serve your gods or worship the image of god you have set up." So there! Take that!

You can imagine that on that note, the king had a harsh reaction to what he viewed as pure nerve on the part of Shadrach, Meshach, and Abednego. He now had no out but to play his hand. His ego was at stake. In his fury he ordered the furnace to be heated to seven times hotter than its usual heat. The guards who took them to the mouth of the furnace were consumed by the heat of the flames! Yet these three Hebrew boys were unscathed. The king could not believe his eyes. How could it be that four were now walking in the midst of the flames when he had only delivered up three? And the fourth looked like the Son of God walking in the midst of them. Calling them to come out of the furnace, the king was stunned to discover that they were no longer bound. They were free and whole. Not even the smell of the smoke had penetrated their clothing. Truly this God they served was greater than any the king ever had the privilege of meeting. The gods that he was acquainted with did not walk or talk. They certainly did not join their subjects in the midst of such dire circumstances. This was the kind of God for whom he, too, would have stood in ardent uncompromise.

After recovering from the incredulity of all that had transpired, Nebuchadnezzar was forced to admit there was no other god like the God of Shadrach, Meshach, and Abed-nego. Suddenly quite zealous about this revelation, he decreed that anyone who had anything to say against their God would be cut into pieces and their houses turned into piles of rubble. How's that for an immediate switch? But then he went a step further and promoted those three unbending Hebrew men. In refusing to bend beneath earthly idols, God had promoted them above principalities. Because principle was greater to them than deliverance or reward, they received it all.

*W*here is the reward in being righteous? we ask ourselves more often than we care to admit. It seems that everyone around us is doing as they please and not suffering any hardship from it. Yet there is a reward for righteousness that extends beyond our own personal space. We can experience salvation, deliverance, and promotion in obedience. Better yet, there is a profound witness that shatters the works of darkness and brings those around us into God's marvelous light as they see our good works that glorify our Father in Heaven. This is our ultimate reward. This is where we invest in our heavenly savings account for an eternal day. Our decisions today affect our tomorrow—and the tomorrows of those around us—in a more profound way than we can ever conceive.

> *Dear Heavenly Father, it is so easy to get caught up in the tide and swept away by the opinions of others. Help me to hold fast to Your Word alone. As I am assaulted with various beliefs and standards, help me to hold on to what You decree concerning every matter. Grant me the discernment and the courage to stand immovable in what I know to be true,*

trusting You to be the defender of my faith. I believe that You are the rewarder of those who diligently seek You; therefore the offerings of men are as nothing in my eyes. In the time when the enemy attempts to make what the world holds dear glitter like gold, help me to see beyond the surface to Your brilliant light that overshadows all. In Jesus' name, amen.

Guilty Times

*And they which heard it, being convicted by their
own conscience, went out one by one, beginning
at the eldest, even unto the last: and Jesus was left alone,
and the woman standing in the midst.*

JOHN 8:9 KJV

Slipping behind the door, she carefully guided it shut with hands laid against its frame as if to shush the bolt from making a sound. She drew a careful breath. Alone at last. When he entered, they clung to each other hungrily, relieved to finally be in one another's arms. This was true solace. A stolen moment. A covert meeting. A much-anticipated tryst. No one would ever know. This was their sweet secret. This was the hour anticipated. And it was every bit as passionate as they had imagined. Or was it just the thrill of the forbidden that heightened their ecstasy? Ah, but they weren't as alone as they thought. Suddenly a sharp sound shattered the moment as shouts of "Adulterer! Adulterer!" filled the air. "I told you we would find them here!" someone shouted as strong and angry hands grasped her roughly in the midst of her struggle to redress herself. Her thoughts were muddled as indignant eyes and pursed lips surrounded her along with threats of stoning as she searched for the eyes of her lover in the crowd. But he had vanished, leaving her to suffer their rebukes alone.

Alone. She couldn't remember ever feeling this alone. There was something about accusations that made you feel naked even when fully dressed. Ashamed. Defenseless. Worthless. Defeated. And so she silently hung her head and endured the embarrassment of being dragged through the center of town, while everyone—eyebrows raised, mouths dropped in dismay, shoulders hunched together, lips preparing to whisper—looked on. The gossipmongers wearing those looks that proclaimed, "I *told* you she was a wicked woman." The shame cut deeper than the pain that came from hands jostling her roughly through the streets, handling her as carelessly as the street cleaners handled spoiled produce that fell from passing pouches. She had almost prepared herself mentally for the first stone to be thrown when she noticed that their steps had slowed in front of the Temple.

She saw His feet first, as her eyes remained fixated on the ground. She could feel the press of the crowd as the hard-handed men pushed her forward. "Rabbi," they announced, "this woman was caught in the very act of adultery. The law of Moses says to stone her. What do you say?" She held her breath. How could she dare hope for redemption now? She was guilty. She knew it. Her captors knew it. And then something happened. All of a sudden she saw Him, not because she had lifted her head, but because He had lowered Himself to the ground beneath her. This man who was supposedly the Son of God, who had descended from heaven to earth for the sins of man, lowered Himself—in front of *her!* She was stunned and confused. What was He doing? He was writing something in the dust that her tear-filled eyes could not decipher. The crowd grew impatient, becoming more menacing and demanding in the face of His seemingly nonchalant posture toward this...this...harlot! And then He stood, once again out of her line of vision, facing her accusers, and spoke—calmly, quietly, effortlessly, as if He were simply breathing out the thought instead of vocalizing it. "All right, stone her. But let those who have never sinned throw the first stones!" He returned within the frame of her view and continued to write in the dust.

The rumbling among the masses stopped abruptly. One by one, their countenances transformed from indignant to uncomfortable. Silently they moved away, until there remained just these two—the lady and her Lord. And then He arose, lifting her eyes to His. She was speechless. His gaze held a gentleness she had not anticipated. She had never felt this way before. She felt as if no one else in the world existed in that space of time, as the eyes of Jesus Himself held her in their grip, flooding her with this strange sense of peace. His voice was like that of a concerned parent trying to soothe a frightened child. "Where are your accusers? Did not even one of them condemn you?" She found her voice to answer, "No, Lord." And then He smiled the most beautiful smile. It reminded her of the quiet splendor of the sun rising over the hills of Jerusalem. "Neither do I. Go and sin no more." Was it relief or tears that bathed her? She could not tell. His words were too good to be true, and she grasped them as if someone had tossed her a bag brimming with silver, clutching them to her breast as she went her way. Redeemed! Forgiven! Not as alone as she thought!

Could forgiveness really be that simple? Why does it seem that when we are surrounded by condemnation, nothing can be said or done to relieve us from the deep and binding guilt we feel? We are seemingly forsaken by our own sense of self. And we imagine that we are forsaken by the One who can redeem us. We find ourselves lost and wandering alone in the forest of our own interpretations of God's judgment upon our lives. As the accuser presses in, he burdens us to the point where we feel as if we couldn't get a prayer through to heaven even if we attached it to a high-powered missile. And then Jesus comes down, lifts our chin in His hand, and gently asks, "You were saying?"

> *Dear Heavenly Father, there are things in my life that I have been reluctant to bring to Your attention. I feared You would agree with my accusers, and yet I feel so alone in my secrecy, trapped by my lack of confession. I have tried to intellectualize the guilt away by rationalizing my sin, but still I feel no relief. My heart is heavy and my peace is gone. Please God, as I confess the things that weigh upon my soul, set me free. Free from the voice of the accuser as well as from my own self-inflicted condemnation. For I realize this is why Jesus died, for such a time as this. I receive His cleansing power now. In Jesus' name, amen.*

Angry Times

*When Pilate saw that he could prevail nothing,
but that rather a tumult was made, he took water,
and washed his hands before the multitude, saying,
I am innocent of the blood of this just person: see ye to it.*

MATTHEW 27:24 KJV

Perspiration ran like rivers under Pilate's armpits. Yet he knew it was not the heat that caused his body to overreact in this manner. It was instead the feeling that he was being involuntarily dragged into yet another affair that he wanted no part of. Pilate wondered what he had done to displease the gods to such an extent that they would banish him to this godforsaken place. Actually, godforsaken was an understatement, for in this region it was their God who seemed to cause all of the problems. Truly, these people were like no other he had ever encountered. They were indescribably different from the people of any other territory the Romans had conquered. Though they had militarily dominated Judea, the people were as out of control as ever. So religious were they, they didn't have the sense to fear those who dominated them with physical force. Pilate was weary. He had tried to do the best he could as governor of this province, yet no matter what he did or didn't do he managed to offend these people more than assuage their restlessness. And now here they were again, demanding that he kill an innocent man.

He found himself calling upon God, or any god that would listen, for mercy. He sat looking into the eyes of this man called Jesus, trying to decipher why the people were so incensed against Him. He looked innocent enough. Yet something about His eyes arrested you and filled you with a strange feeling. There was a peace about Him that was almost disconcerting in the midst of all the chaos. He was...too cool. The thought made Pilate perspire even more. As he sat trying to reason with the people, someone brought him a note from his wife. Although it was unlike her to meddle in his official affairs, even she had been disturbed by this latest case. She moved to advise him against being involved in this man's crucifixion. Perhaps if he stacked the deck against their demands by asking them to choose between an obvious criminal and this Jesus who was clearly innocent, they would help him slip out of this volatile situation. He could not afford to be reported to the emperor at this point. Let their conscience make the decision for him. Surely if they feared God, they would let Jesus go. But this idea was quickly foiled as they chose to release Barabbas, the criminal, and crucify Jesus, the innocent.

What strange people they were, he thought again. *How could they be so callous?* Pilate concluded that surely their religion was one of convenience, for no one who was truly spiritual could be so hateful. He might not be the most religious person in the world, but he did have a conscience. A sense of right and wrong. And no matter how much they screamed or tried to manipulate him to give them permission to kill this man, he knew he could not live in peace with Jesus' blood on his hands. He found their willingness to absorb the guilt of His death shocking. After all, what had He done? So what if He claimed to be the Son of God. They should just chalk it up to madness and move on. But these people lived by the letter of the law—a law Pilate found far too stringent, yet strangely flexible when held in the hands of the high priests. It was amazing how they twisted these things to get their way. But never mind—none of this was his business. As he washed his hands to demonstrate that he was immune from their decision, he felt more than the film of the dust of Jerusalem leave him. It was as if he had plunged his soul into the cool water in the basin. Perhaps God thought him worthy of sparing, after all. He didn't understand everything he felt at that moment. He only knew he would be one of very few who would sleep in peace that night. Yes, it was a job, and he had to make a living, but not at the expense of his soul.

Who are you listening to? Voices are powerful things. Especially when you are one in the face of many. Especially when your financial or job security is involved. They can be intimidating, fearsome, convincing, and overwhelming as they entice you to go with the flow. To not rock the boat and bring unwanted attention to yourself. To be singled out as someone who's difficult. It's very tempting to go against your best instincts when everyone around is screaming for you to go in the opposite direction of your heart. The crowd of popular opinion makes it hard to hear the Holy Spirit and yet He speaks, saying, "This is the way, walk ye in it." Though we might not feel that we are especially spiritual or that we even come close to measuring up in the eyes of God, the Holy Spirit still proves to be a faithful companion to those who have lost their way. His instructions are light on our path and lead us to a place of righteousness, peace, and joy. His words, though they may be contrary to the words of the masses, always direct us toward decisions that keep us free from being separated from the will and presence of our Heavenly Father while holding intact all that is key to our security and well-being.

> *Dear Heavenly Father, hold me close so that I might hear Your whisper above all the shouting. Silence my flesh so that I might hear Your Spirit. In spite of my lack of understanding, let my trust in You outweigh my tendency to second-guess You. Still my heart and calm me. Strengthen my resolve to be obedient to You no matter what I see, hear, or think. Order my steps, direct my path, and keep me on Your way. May the enemy's design to entrap and confuse me be thwarted. I trust You to keep all that concerns me safe from the reach of those who would threaten to rob or destroy me. Keep me walking in the liberty of Your divine direction. In Jesus' name, amen.*

Violent Times

When they heard this, they were furious and gnashed
their teeth at him. But Stephen, full of the Holy Spirit,
looked up to heaven and saw the glory of God,
and Jesus standing at the right hand of God.

ACTS 7:54

Pity, sadness, unwavering conviction...anything
but the rage these people were expressing washed over
Stephen as he listened to their accusations. He knew they
were all lies; his conscience was clear before God, and
that was all that mattered. The people didn't want to know
the truth. They wanted to continue in their way, and so be
it. It was not Stephen's job to convince them, but it certainly was his call to speak the truth in love and leave
them to decide whether they chose life or death, blessings
or cursings. The calmness of his countenance enraged his
accusers even more. How dare he be so smug, so confident! Did he think he was God too, as this Jesus that he
spoke of had been known to claim? Since He too had
wrought miracles and always seemed to have an answer
for every argument concerning Scripture, had Stephen

likewise gotten too big for his britches and judged himself to be superior over them? If that was the case, they would show him.

And so they gazed at him intently, waiting for him to break beneath the pressure of their stares. But Stephen was silent. "Are these charges true? Have you been speaking blasphemy against Moses and God?" the high priests asked. Perhaps they should not have asked this question, for they now opened the door to a monologue they did not want to hear. As Stephen recounted the history of the Israelites and their consistently rebellious behavior toward God, their consciences cut them to the quick, making thin and precise incisions into their spirits like painful paper cuts. They screamed in pain and ground their teeth, so intense was their hatred of this man who forced them to deal with issues that required more of themselves than they were willing to give. They covered their ears to shut out his voice, but now his words were in their heads, ringing in their spirits. They shouted to drown out the questions that were beginning to rise from their inward parts. The more they shouted, the calmer he became. And that, of course, stirred them to uncontrollable heights of madness.

But Stephen was too busy looking beyond where he stood. He gazed far past the incensed crowd with their contorted, scowling faces and pointed his face toward the heavenlies. As the Holy Spirit came and filled him to overflowing, he felt almost cocooned in the embrace of God, insulated from the threats of the angry crowd. Nothing mattered now. Nothing mattered in the light of the glory he was beholding. Jesus Himself was standing! Not sitting, but standing up on Stephen's behalf! The awesomeness of what he saw was overwhelming; surely his Redeemer lived and cared for him. In the face of human hatred, Stephen was overshadowed by something greater—divine love. What he felt could not be contained within him. He wanted everyone to see what he saw, and it burst from his lips: "Look, I see the heavens opened and the Son of Man standing in the place of honor at God's right hand."

The people could not believe Stephen's audacity. They could think of only one way to resolve the feelings he had stirred up within them. He must be silenced once and for all. They rushed upon him, dragging him through the city. The stones they held in their hands gave them relief as they hurled them in his direction. And still he stood unflinching. Was there nothing that would make this man bow? Even as he sank to his knees giving in to death, he prayed, "Lord Jesus, receive my spirit; don't charge them with this sin." And with that he died. What they sought as relief would now become the very thing that haunted them in their dreams, in their every waking moment. For his death sealed everything that they had said. He was no longer there, available to ease the pressure by revoking his report. He had willingly given his life for what he believed. His conviction was sealed and inescapable, especially to one called Saul.

Nothing in the kingdom's economy is

a waste. Every life is accounted for

and bears great meaning.

How could any good come from such rage? We often view the premature death of someone as a waste and a tragedy. But nothing in the kingdom's economy is a waste. Every life is accounted for and bears great meaning. Every soul is an investment in another. Where is God when we stand accused for His sake? He is standing. Standing as we stand. As we guard His interests, He covers ours and gives us the grace we need to stand unmovable in the face of opposition. Even as we die inside from the lack of a ready reception from others, God fills in the empty places with His Own Spirit and His gracious approval of our faithfulness. Saul was among those who stoned Stephen and paved the way for waves of persecution toward all Christians in the coming times. But out of persecution an even greater wave of revival arose as others fled to safer havens, taking the Good News with them, accompanied by signs, wonders, and miracles. It was in this atmosphere that the gospel was spread abroad, even to parts of Africa, and Saul was converted. His name was changed to Paul, and he amazingly went on to write a major part of the New Testament. This proves the point that we never know who is watching us and how our life might affect others. God is able to use it all. What we view as the end is only the beginning from God's viewpoint. Our lives and testaments are merely seeds that the Holy Spirit waters, while God is faithful to glean the increase. No life is ever in vain when it is a life lived for God.

> *Dear Heavenly Father, though life is dear, You are dearer. As I render myself to Your service, help me to do so uncompromisingly. Let the words of my mouth and the meditation of my heart always be acceptable in Your sight. As Your perfect love casts out all fear in me, make me a vessel of Your truth. Though the world rages against what You require of us all, help me to stand, unwavering in the face of argument, always having an answer for the faith that lies within me. In the face of hostility let Your presence and support be my comfort. In Jesus' name, amen.*

Faithful Times

*The angel answered, "Your prayers and gifts to the poor
have come up as a memorial offering before God."*

ACTS 10:4

Cornelius bustled around the corner, rubbing his hands in thankfulness. *Poor family*, he thought, yet he was grateful he had something to give them. The Roman centurion felt sad that the Jewish people lived in such opposition to the Romans. Of course, many of his people *had* done terrible things to reinforce the Jews' attitude against them. They were always mildly set off-balance when he extended kindness to them, yet Cornelius felt compelled to be arms of healing to those who had been so deeply wounded. He had come to learn of their God and embraced Him fully. The times of his life that he treasured most were those spent in prayer, in quiet times reflecting who this God was that the Jews struggled to keep to themselves. It was almost as if they were members of an exclusive club, and no one but the Israelites could get into it to worship their God. Cornelius could not go past the outer court of the temple. This was the place reserved for the Gentiles, yet the Jews had dismissed the idea that some Gentiles indeed might want to pray there. So they turned it into a common marketplace, selling their wares under the guise of furnishing everything one would need in order to offer a suitable sacrifice. But it was business—pure and simple. So Cornelius chose the sanctuary of his own home to worship, hoping that this exclusive God would have mercy on Him and grant him visitation.

And so it was at this very moment as Cornelius looked up that he encountered an angel of God standing before him. He was overcome with fear. Had he offended this God, daring to call upon Him when His attention was reserved for the Jews alone? What would be his punishment? Indeed, it must be severe—He had dispatched an angel to tend to him! Yet the angel bore the most incredible news. Though he had been unable to offer sacrifices and offerings at the temple, all of Cornelius' prayers and acts of generosity had risen before God as a memorial offering! He was to send for one Simon Peter, who resided in Joppa, to come to his house. Bustling off to send his servants on their way, Cornelius vibrated with anticipation. He had heard of Peter and the other disciples. He was anxious to see what they would share with his household. Though his entire house was devout, he knew that a prophet was not appreciated in his own home. So he prayed that this man, Simon Peter, would come bearing news that would take their faith to another level beyond what his limited teaching had provided.

And so the household of Cornelius stood awaiting what Peter, who now stood before them looking slightly uncomfortable, had to say. He seemed hesitant to share his Lord with them, and he confessed that God had confronted him with this very issue. He told them that God

Himself had instructed him not to call any man impure or unclean. And Cornelius replied that he and his house were ready to hear what God had to say to them. As Peter unfolded the testimony of walking and talking with Jesus, of witnessing His crucifixion and His resurrection, the entire household was moved as they had never been moved before. Peter's words bathed their souls. It was as if layers of filthy clothing were being removed from them even as he spoke. And then the Holy Spirit came upon them, and they glorified God. It was an explosive, electrically charged atmosphere, and even Peter had to bear witness to the fact that the gospel could no longer be contained by just the Jews. The God they served was bigger than that, embracing all people. He would not ignore anyone who called upon Him no matter what race, what creed, what gender they were. To Him they were not Greek or Jew, male or female—just a soul He longed to welcome as His own. He was the rewarder of all who diligently sought Him, ready and willing to meet all who came to Him in contrition and humility, bearing offerings that came from the heart.

In what areas do you feel insufficient in your walk before God? It is such a relief to know that God is not a religious God bound by the rules of men. That He looks beyond the surface of who we are, what we do, and even how we choose to give honor to Him. His eyes pass the external as the Holy Spirit judges the inner parts, seeking a heart that desires to serve Him above all things. This is the one He embraces. He isn't angry if you are not crossing all of your spiritual *t*'s and dotting your religious *i*'s; your simple prayers and acts of kindness to others have come up as a memorial before the Lord. He sees the intent of your heart and rewards you accordingly. The standards of men and what qualify as worship are not the same to Him, for He merely seeks worshipers who glorify Him in spirit and in truth. This is a simpler place to be than most religious folk would like to presume, yet God acknowledges all who come to Him out of the pure intent of their hearts. This is enough for Him.

> *Dear Heavenly Father, I come to You bearing nothing but my repentant heart and the need to know You in all Your glory. Fill me with Yourself to overflowing. As I yield myself to You, make me a sanctuary for Your spirit. Dwell in the midst of my heart and instruct me in Your ways. Fill my mouth with Your praises and all that delights You. Remember my need for Your grace and mercy. As I extend my arms to others, may Your presence in my life be evident, and let everything I do further glorify Your name. I pray in Jesus' name, amen.*

Revolutionary Times

Then took they up stones to cast at him:
but Jesus hid himself, and went out of the temple,
going through the midst of them, and so passed by.

JOHN 8:59 KJV

⁂

he faces before Jesus were mere masks that He looked through as He surveyed the indignant crowd. Their hearts were cesspools of rebellion and legalistic rationale. If He had not been long prepared for their waywardness, Jesus would have found this conversation in the temple most disconcerting. How could those who claimed to seek God and pored over the scriptures intently have such a lack of understanding? Yet He already knew the answer. They weren't interested in what God had to say unless it added credence to their own beliefs and personal agendas. So rather than take the Word of God at face value, exactly as written, they puffed up their own self-importance with lofty dissertations that had nothing to do with what God originally said. They wanted to play God's game by their own rules, and they twisted it to meet their own requirements. Now here He was disrupting their religious program by telling the truth.

Oh, and what truths they were! They were shocked and appalled by His claims. He had come from God! Who exactly did He think He was? And how dare He say that they were the children of the devil, slaves to sin? And even more preposterous, He said that He knew Abraham! Oh, it looked like there was no shame in this "Son of Man"—whatever that expression meant! He was a troublemaker, always going against the grain, interfering where He shouldn't. Who died and crowned Him king? Who gave Him the authority to forgive adulterers, to heal on the Sabbath, and to claim to know more than they all knew? They had been in the temple long before He arrived on the scene. They knew where He came from, and His background was not very impressive. After all, what good could come out of Nazareth? He was still young—early thirties, they assumed. Where did He get off thinking He knew so much? It had taken them a lifetime to decipher the laws of Moses, and now He came barging in claiming to be an authority! He was calling them liars and warning them of their eternal fate. Telling them their attitudes were all wrong and that they were an ungodly generation.

This was just too much for them to take in. It upset the beliefs they had settled into, raised too many uncomfortable questions. It confronted the darkness of their hearts and their selfish agendas. It violated their pride and assaulted their self-esteem. The things He spoke of demanded change on their part, changes they were unwilling to make. They were content to find the fault in others that soothed their own sore consciences. It was a comfort to know that worse sinners than themselves were always out there to be found. How dare He come and challenge them to be accountable? His superior manner would simply not be tolerated! As they moved to pick up stones to silence Him, they grew even more frustrated, for He had vanished.

Vanished! They could neither lay hands on Him theologically nor physically. None of their manipulations worked. Though they continued to lay traps for Him, He continued to escape every snare. He was blameless—they knew it, and this incensed them against Him even more. But nothing could be done until He chose to deliver Himself into their hands. Many times He eluded them, explaining that "My time has not come." Wrapped in the covering of God's purpose, He was not exposed to the whims of men. He was untouched by the stones they hurled against the uprightness of His soul, the crucifixion of His character, or the humiliation of His standards. For He knew who He was. He was acquainted with His purpose. So for the joy that was set before Him, He endured it all surrounded by the hedge of protection provided by His Father.

How freely do you find yourself sharing what you truly believe? This is a time when, as never before, people are refusing to endure sound doctrine. Turn on any talk show or sit in on any conversation within or without the church. The views expressed on moral issues will cause alarm in your soul. *Truly the world is going mad,* we think to ourselves. How can others come to such unbelievable conclusions— and in such a defiant manner? Add to the mix someone prepared to take the Word of God at face value and uphold His principles, and you've got the chemistry going for a Molotov cocktail—there's sure to be an explosion! With this state of affairs, we're often tempted to run the gamut of extremes—from saying, "Why bother? No one is listening anyway," to becoming overly obnoxious in defense of our faith. The key is to find the place of graciousness that Jesus possessed. It was not *how* He said what He said. It was *what* He said that offended their spiritual senses. We must be ever mindful to walk in the Spirit, being aware of when our "time has come." Covered in the security of who we are in Him. Knowing full well our destination based on His heavenly purpose. No longer subject to the flesh but answering to a higher call that places us above our natural circumstances, no matter how volatile. In this we find lasting victory. For though the crowd rages, God is greater than the masses of those who hold only the threat of harming the flesh. They have no power over the soul.

> *Dear Heavenly Father, my complete reliance is on You. You are my help and my strength in the face of men's opposition. Arise, O God, let my enemies be scattered. Help me find my hiding place beneath Your wings. Lord, I choose to rest in the knowledge that You are a shield about me as I fix my face to do Your bidding. When tempted to defend myself, let me be reminded that You are my defense. Remind me that You have accounted for all my days and are determined to complete the work that You've begun in me. As you allow my righteousness to shine forth as the noonday sun, free me from the condemnation of others and keep me ever in the center of Your will. In Jesus' name, amen.*

In the Heart
of the
Inner Journey

Isolation is necessary for Intimacy,
Intimacy is necessary for Impartation,
Impartation is necessary for Change.

MIKE MURDOCK

Brooding Times

In the beginning God created the heavens and the earth.
The earth was empty, a formless mass cloaked in darkness.
And the Spirit of God was hovering over its surface.

GENESIS 1:1,2 NLT

God sighed. It was a sigh like no other, for it revealed the heart of this Omnipotent God. The Alpha and Omega. The Beginning and the End. The One who had always been because He had always existed within Himself desired companionship. Though the heavenly host was in constant attendance, something was missing. Lucifer had left a tremendous gap after he was banished from the heavens for his rebellion. And though it was God's decision that this worker of iniquity depart from His presence, it did not lessen the pain He felt of losing not only one He considered a "son of the morning," but also a third of the angelic host. The absence of their voices, their praise and worship, left a void in the heavenlies. And that space grew even more immense with time. Yes, God was lonely. Lonely for those who would worship Him in spirit and in truth. Though praises rang constantly in His throne room, something was lacking. A note was missing from the harmony being sounded. It had sounded before but now it was gone; its absence was felt.

Never again would He make anything like Lucifer. He had made him perfect in every way, the most beautiful of all the angels, so beautiful that he had grown haughty at his own reflection. No, this time He would create man. An even more awesome creation than anything He had made in the heavenlies because he would be formed in His own image! Reflecting His likeness. This man would walk in perfect fellowship with Him. Fearfully and wonderfully made, he would be one who was like Him, created to fellowship with Him intimately. No longer would God place one in charge of gathering the worship and praise unto Him. Each man would come bearing his own chorus of praise. And the man would have access to bring his praise before God personally.

He considered the risks involved, mapping out the compensation for every weakness that this man would have. He knew that His greatest desire would also call for His greatest sacrifice, but still it would be worth it. Worth it to reclaim that note, that missing note that resonated in His soul. Life as it presently existed was like an unfinished symphony, lacking the sound of intimate worship flowing from a willing heart and creating its own sweet perfume. Heavy like incense, lingering long after the last chord had been echoed. And so, as all of heaven held its breath, God set to work. First He prepared a place for him to live. Not being made from the same substance as those in heaven, man would not be able to survive up there. He must be made from his surroundings in order to subsist.

Pondering all these details, God gazed down at Earth. He looked past the sphere, now dark and void, to light years beyond, knowing all that would transpire once He chose to fill it with life. "Let there be light!" He said, and the lights went on, warming the face of the frozen ball, melting the ice that covered it. And God separated the waters from the earth, furnishing this paradise with all sorts of incredible living things. But He saved His best creation for last— man himself. God gazed at this perfect wonder lying so peacefully still, one with the ground from which he was made. Ever so tenderly, He bent down and breathed into him the breath of life. Man became a living soul.

What pleasure this creation brought to God's heart! He anticipated their conversations in the cool of the evening. They were friends, exchanging freely. And yet He knew He could not keep Adam all to Himself. To do this would be to deny His own nature which demanded that He give—because that's what love does. It was not good for Adam to be alone, as it had not been good for God Himself to be filled with such longing for the heart of another. So He fashioned for man an extension of himself, which He called woman.

But then one day the wonderfulness was marred. The moment it happened, the heavens reverberated from the cold air of separation that suddenly cut like a knife through the stratosphere. A note went sour in the midst of the chorus and God rose up to go down and see what had taken place for Himself. Keeping His usual evening appointment with the man and the woman, He found the garden strangely silent. And in His knowing He grew deeply sad. It had begun. The saga of all that He had foreseen had started. With this knowledge He made a sacrifice to cover their shame. He ached at the thought of the consequences their actions invoked because, in spite of their disobedience, He still loved them, still longed for their fellowship and worship. As He watched them leave the garden, He was already longing for the day when they would be able to return once again.

How do you deal with the pain of missing one you love? We have all experienced loving someone who offended us either consciously or unconsciously. Someone who chose not to love us back. We've felt the sting of separation and longed for restoration. It seems that, in their absence, the memories of our times together are magnified, leaving an even greater feeling of longing. This should give us an indication of how God longs after us. How wonderful to be able to rest in the fact that we can release all we are to Him and never, ever suffer from rejection. We love Him because He first loved us. We didn't choose Him; He chose us! He is so determined to embrace us that He promises that nothing shall ever separate us from His love. He calls us to be reconciled to Him through the shed blood of His Son, Jesus Christ. Through the blood we find our way back to the garden where we once again can stand before God, naked and unashamed.

> *Dear Heavenly Father, I come to You seeking total restoration with You. Today I would like to reestablish a love covenant between us. I ask that You take my filthy garments and wash them white as snow. I want to stand before You completely whole and unashamed, free to share all that I am with You. Thank You for first loving me. Thank You for giving Your Son just for me. Teach me how to walk in a way that is pleasing to You. Show me how to worship You in spirit and in truth, that I might fulfill my purpose and bring pleasure to Your heart. As I seek to draw closer to You, meet me and unfold Your nature and Your ways to me that I might grow ever more intimate with You as I increase in the knowledge of who You are. In Jesus' name, amen.*

Rejected Times

Thereafter, Hagar referred to the Lord,
who had spoken to her, as "the God who sees me,"
for she said, "I have seen the One who sees me!"

GENESIS 16:13 NLT

hat was she to do now? This was a fine mess she had gotten herself into. And yet Hagar found it hard to absorb the blame for all that had transpired. She had been minding her own business doing her maidly duties. It was Sarah who had suggested that her master Abraham sleep with her. Hagar had not volunteered for this attention. But Sarah, who had grown weary of waiting for the Lord to open her womb, had chosen her maid to be a surrogate mother and produce an heir for Abraham. And so she had complied.

The change in Sarah was immediate upon learning of Hagar's pregnancy. Sarah accused her of being contemptuous toward her. This was simply not true in Hagar's mind. She merely wanted to be treated with a little respect. After all, she *was* bearing Abraham's child. A bit of deference was the least she deserved! She must admit that she did feel a strange rush of power, and it expanded as the child grew within her. How fortunate she was. Who would have ever thought that this little Egyptian maidservant would end up bearing the heir apparent to this wealthy man? Truly the gods had smiled on her, or perhaps it was Abraham's God. She wasn't sure, for she wasn't acquainted with Him. She couldn't help it if Sarah chose to feel insecure. That wasn't her problem. Like it or not, Hagar was the one with the child. Sarah would just have to deal with it.

But that was not the way it went at all. Sarah had grown increasingly harsh with her maid, and Abraham did not intervene at all. As Hagar's body went through the changes of pregnancy and her emotions ran the gamut as her system adjusted to the new life inside of her, the caustic barbs of her mistress made life unbearable. Perhaps this had not been a blessing after all, but a curse. How could she live in the midst of such immense jealousy and resentment? Why wouldn't Abraham come to her defense? And would her child also be subject to such cruel treatment? That was the last straw; Hager would never allow that to happen. And with that she ran away. Away from the constant bickering. Away from Abraham's weariness and weak apologies on behalf of his wife. Away from what she was certain would become a difficult environment for her child.

As she rested beside a desert spring along the road to Shur, trying to decide exactly which direction she desired to travel, an angel of the Lord approached her. He gently questioned what purpose she had for being in this place, and she replied that she was running away from her mistress. Surely the angel would see her side of the story. But instead he gently corrected her, telling her that she should return to her mistress and submit to her. Along with the correction came an incredible promise—she would have more descendants than she could count. She would give birth to a son and name him Ishmael, for the Lord had heard about her misery. The Lord had heard about her misery! This God whom she had not acknowledged, knowing little to nothing about Him, cared enough to acknowledge her state of being, the bitterness of her soul!

Somehow knowing that God saw and cared made her able to deal with her circumstance. Yes, she would return to her mistress. She would submit, come what may. She could endure Sarah's cutting remarks and rough treatment, for God had seen her misery. He had made her a personal promise. She would not look for a reward from Abraham or any other man. Her reward would come from God. "He is the One who sees me." These words rang in her heart all the way back home. They rang in her heart every time Sarah tried to ruffle her feathers and remind her of her subordinate stature. They rang in her spirit as she delivered her son, Ishmael, "God Hears." As she looked into the beautiful face of her newborn son, she saw the future promises of God in his eyes. Truly He had seen Hagar and heard the cry of her heart. This was beyond her expectations. This became the most humbling gift of all.

Is there a place in your life that could use a little humility? We all have a tendency to go on a power trip from time to time, getting a little too big for our britches or enjoying a bit of one-upsmanship when a situation turns in our favor in the presence of someone who previously bested us. But we need to be careful about doing this. Whether the one in authority over us is right or wrong, we must still remain in a place of submission. Because the more we rebel, the more the one in charge will tighten the screws on us. At that point we've become so focused on their attitude that we don't deal with our own. We wonder why God won't come to our defense and deal with this mean person who is bent on making our life difficult. Then, as we stop to catch our breath from the exertion of all our effort, God reminds us that we must first be obedient to His Word; He will take care of the rest. As we work as unto Him, in a stance of submission, He will bless us. He has seen our misery, He has heard our cry, and He has a promise for us that will make up for all that we have been through. But first we must return to Him and yield to His instruction.

> *Dear Heavenly Father, I confess my wrong attitude*
> *to You. I lay my rebellious heart before You and ask*
> *that You give me a clean heart and renew a right*
> *spirit within me. Help me to look past the present cir-*
> *cumstance to see Your promises. Help me to hear*
> *beyond the remarks that cut, wound, and discourage.*
> *I want to hear the real need in the lives of those that*
> *You've placed over me in authority. As I walk softly*
> *before them, working as unto You, regard my situa-*
> *tion and let not my enemies triumph over me. Lift*
> *me up and wrap me in Your peace. Let Your peace*
> *be my peace as I keep my eyes on You, knowing that*
> *You see and hear all. I know that You care for me*
> *and in this knowledge I will wait for Your*
> *redemption. In Jesus' name, amen.*

The valley and my heart are one
as I search for love
deep and unending
I find no stair to climb
my feet are soaked
from the rain of my tears
as I stroll through my longings
becoming drenched in the rejection of others
and You come
gently covering me as I begin
to sink in the mire of my loneliness
You come replacing all that was before
folding me inside Your heart
carrying me to the mountaintop
where I see light at the end of my desires...

Lonely Times

But because Leah was unloved, the Lord let her have a child,
while Rachel was childless. So Leah became pregnant and
had a son. She named him Reuben, for she said, "The Lord
has noticed my misery, and now my husband will love me."

GENESIS 29:31,32 NLT

With a sinking heart, Leah watched Jacob going toward Rachel's tent. Every step he took cut her like a knife, going deeper and deeper into her soul. All she wanted was his love. Was that such a difficult request? Yet she continued to feel like an unwelcome intrusion in Jacob's life. He came to her out of duty, not desire. The entire time his mind was elsewhere. She could literally see the separation of his body and soul when he was with her. All she longed for was to see the same light in Jacob's eyes that shone when he looked toward Rachel.

Leah shrugged her shoulders and went into her tent. What should she expect? How silly of her—she had thought things would be different after she was married to Jacob. When he first arrived, she had hoped that finally the Lord had delivered a husband to her. But instead he had set his affections upon Rachel, her younger sister. Rachel was all that Jacob saw, and he vowed to work seven years for her hand. And why not? Rachel was beautiful while she, Leah, was nothing to write home about. But that didn't mean she was any less of a woman than Rachel. No less capable of loving him and becoming all that a man could hope for. Yet she had been overlooked. Her sadness had grown deeper as Rachel's wedding day approached. The disgrace of her younger sister being married before she was married was oppressive and draining. And then her father had given her a glimpse of hope. He had approached her, telling her she would be the one in Jacob's marriage tent that night. She was not to utter a word. "Don't worry about anything," he said. "It will all work out." She didn't really think he would let her younger sister get married before her, did she? She asked him what Rachel would think, and he answered that Rachel would do as she was told; that was not her concern. The immediate mission at hand was to get Leah married. That was what she wanted, too, wasn't it?

She had been so nervous that night as she waited for Jacob. What if he noticed right away that she wasn't Rachel and refused to consummate their union? She held her breath as he entered the tent, giddy from the wine of the celebration. Selfishness assuaged her guilt as he began to caress her; she told herself that it didn't matter that he called Rachel's name instead of hers over and over again. All that mattered was that he belonged to her. In time, his heart would change when he saw that she could love him and give him pleasure, too.

But daylight brought harsh reality, dispelling the shadows that harbored her heart's desire. Jacob was furious to find that he had been tricked. He glared at Leah in anger. His unspoken accusations of betrayal hurt more than any words he could have uttered. Rachel, too, had shunned her, distressed that her own sister could so willingly go along with her father's deceit. Didn't anybody care how Leah felt? She was the one who had been manipulated. How could she refuse to obey her father? Didn't Rachel understand that she, unlike Leah, would have no problem getting a husband because of her great beauty? What kind of sister would want to rob her sibling of her one grasp at happiness? This was Leah's only chance. Who could blame her for taking it? For daring to hope she could get a little contentment out of the deal? But instead she was now more miserable than before. Her feelings of rejection heightened in the face of Jacob's disdain. She had never imagined that the loneliness of being single was far less painful than the loneliness of an unhappy marriage. She could do nothing to win Jacob's heart. He still loved Rachel, and he gladly worked another seven years to have her by his side.

What is it that makes a man love a woman like that? Leah wondered to herself. After all, Rachel often acted more than a bit spoiled. She was used to having her way, taking for granted the many opportunities that beauty brings. Leah, on the other hand, had to depend on the goodness of her ways to make up for her physical deficits. Shouldn't that account for something? And where was God in all of this? It just wasn't fair. She was a victim in the middle of this drama, and no one seemed to understand how she felt. No one understood and no one cared. Or so she thought. But then the Lord opened her womb! She waited, holding her newborn son in her arms, for Jacob to enter the tent. "Perhaps my husband will love me now," she thought. She looked for the light of love, some glint of affectionate approval from him. But all she got was a grunt acknowledging a job well done, she had given him a son, but that was all. In time she learned that he viewed her pregnancies as a good excuse not to share her bed and instead stay with Rachel. With each child Leah bore, her only hope was that her husband would love her for the gift she gave him. Her only comfort was that Rachel had no children. Perhaps God had chosen to look favorably upon her, after all.

Upon the birth of her fourth son, Leah had a revelation. God had been her only constant through all this emotional trauma. He had neither asked for nor taken anything. He had made no judgment of her one way or the other. And He most certainly had not rejected her. He had chosen to fill her life with love by granting her children who filled the void her husband had left vacant. This time Leah chose not to look to her husband for affirmation, but to acknowledge the One who had always loved her. "This time I will praise the Lord," she said, and named her child Judah, which meant "praise." Six sons and one daughter later, a maturity began to fill in the edges of Leah's world and quieted her longing for Jacob's love. The contest between sisters was over, and God had His own way of making everyone a winner. Truly it was easier to rest in the contentment He offered than to continue struggling in the flesh for rewards that could not be contained by human hands. What she was seeking all along had to be birthed not from the external attentions of others, but from within the soul.

*We have been fashioned in such a way
that no external element is able to do
what the Holy Spirit specializes in
doing within.*

Do you ever battle with self-doubt? One of the most powerful scriptures in the Bible is, "We love Him because He first loved us." How much energy do we put into striving for the attention, affection, approval, and love of others? We have a tendency to think that if someone would give us a stamp validating us as desirable, we would finally be whole. But the truth is that no one can make us whole if we are not already fulfilled within ourselves. The only one capable of giving us the fulfillment we desire is God Himself. Nobody else can bear the weight of being all that we need them to be. Nobody else is capable of filling all the empty spaces in our spirit. We have been fashioned in such a way that no external element is able to do what the Holy Spirit specializes in doing within. When we release others from doing what our heart demands, God will come in to meet our expectation with gifts more fulfilling than we ever dreamed.

Dear Heavenly Father, forgive me for ignoring You and seeking my comfort from others. Help me to find my fulfillment in You rather than in those who can never deliver like You do. Fill me with Yourself and teach me how to rest in the comfort of Your arms. Turn my eyes toward You so I can see Your immense love for me. Silence the lie of the enemy in my ears that says I am not desirable, that points to my experiences of rejection to further confirm that I am not wanted or loved. Remind me in those times that You loved me enough to sacrifice Your only Son for me. You love me enough to send me a Comforter who is constantly present and sensitive to my every need. Teach me how to bask in Your love and find it to be more than enough to fill every space in my soul. In Jesus' name I pray, amen.

Shameful Times

*Then Miriam and Aaron spoke against Moses
because of the Ethiopian woman whom he had married.*

NUMBERS 12:14,15 NKJV

Moses' wife watched the rumors circulate back to her husband, and she felt his pain. She hated being the source of contention; never did she want to cause any problems for him. Yet she didn't understand these people. She had never seen such murmuring and complaining among her own. She felt so blessed to be married to Moses. He was so kind. So humble. He was a good man, ruling fairly even when the people chose to be difficult. She had seen him crying out to God, and she had seen God answer him faithfully. She had chosen to embrace her husband's God after witnessing all of the marvelous miracles He had done for His people. But now she felt sad. She was an outsider. She was not one of them, and they made sure she and Moses knew it. Their words were hurtful. They questioned the leadership of Moses because of his wife, and she felt it was most unfair.

Within her she felt a nagging restlessness. *What is the deeper issue?* she wondered. Were they jealous of Moses' relationship with God, and, finding no fault in his leadership, had resorted simply playing up the one thing they considered a blemish in his life? As their prejudice rose to the surface she wondered with amazement how this could happen. They of all people knew what it was like to be oppressed and rejected because of their race, didn't they? She herself had not experienced slavery; she was a free woman who simply loved her husband and chose to leave her own culture to be with him. *How quickly we forget,* she thought. But this brought up a greater question. *They* were the ones with access to God. Aaron was a priest and Miriam a prophetess. If they felt this way about her, did God feel the same? Did He consider her an outsider because she was black? How could a God so great be so small if this were the case?

But Moses' wife soon found out that God's heart was very different from the hearts of Aaron and Miriam. God was not pleased with them. His anger burned against Aaron and Miriam as He rebuked them soundly. As He departed from them, Miriam was stricken with leprosy. Moses' wife found this rather ironic. How interesting that God would choose to give Miriam a taste of her own medicine! Miriam had judged someone on the basis of her skin, and now she must see how it felt to be separated and cast off because of what her skin looked like. Moses' wife watched Miriam in sympathy as she left the camp, no longer allowed to dwell within it because of her unclean condition. She knew how that felt, and she would never wish it upon others. Now Miriam would know too. Moses had told her that God had spit in the prophetess' face, so great was His distaste for her attitude. Moses' wife prayed for Miriam as they waited for her to return before they moved on. Because of the intercession of Moses, Miriam would only suffer from this condition for seven days.

Truly Miriam should appreciate God's kindness. Moses' wife chuckled to herself. Poor Miriam—she probably thought it an awful punishment to be a prisoner of her skin for seven days, while *she* would remain different from the others all the days of her life. There was no simple solution for her. She would always encounter the ignorance and insensitive cruelty of others. But perhaps this was why she was so strong. She was bound to rely on the grace and favor of God in a world that would not always be kind. A world that was quick to judge and draw conclusions based on the color of one's skin. But on this day she was strangely comforted. God had spoken to her by His actions. He cared for her. He knew her pain intimately. He would be her advocate and her comforter, her defense and her strength.

Is your heart full of acceptance for others? Fear presses strange buttons within all of us, causing us to recoil from others for all the wrong reasons. We are reluctant to embrace anything different from the norm, yet God says that everything He creates is fearfully and wonderfully made. It's all good! He celebrates our uniqueness. He designed us in all shapes, sizes, and colors *on purpose*. He is a God of variety. He looks upon us all and sees an incredibly exquisite bouquet, one He was willing to pay an expensive price for. So when we choose to insult each other, God takes the insult personally. How dare one cause separation where He has decreed reconciliation! Reconciliation to one another and to Himself. Prejudice has no place in the kingdom. This grieves the Spirit of God, and it is not a matter that He allows to slide. He metes out judgment in the measure the offender serves up. But this is not where it ends. Even as the victims of offense grieve, God takes their pain to heart and draws close with empathetic arms to make His love and His presence known.

> *Dear Heavenly Father, I've been hurt by times when I have been the victim of other people's judgments and assumptions. It is painful—the cut is deep, and I find it hard to forgive in these moments. I ask that You insulate my heart and strengthen me that I might always superimpose Your love over the cruelty of others. Help my self-esteem not to be measured by what others think of me, but rather by what You think of me. I pray that as I walk through this life, I will be secure in You in the face of every encounter, and that my foundation for love and self-acceptance will be grounded in You and Your proclamation over Your creation. I am fearfully and wonderfully made, deliberately crafted by Your hand to be exactly what and who I am, and "it is good." In Jesus' name I pray, amen.*

You are the friend that sticketh
closer than a brother,
lover,
father or mother,
for when I want to reach out to You
I need look no further
than my own soul
where You dwell
rising at every invitation
to greet me...
I wonder why I ignore You so long
seeking You in the faces
and arms of others
when all along You've been
right here,
nearer than I thought
nearer than I ever dreamed...

Unaffirmed Times

"But the people broke in and said to Saul, 'Should Jonathan, who saved Israel today, die? Far from it! As surely as the LORD lives, not one hair on his head will be touched, for he has been used of God to do a mighty miracle today.' So the people rescued Jonathan, and he was not put to death."

1 SAMUEL 14:45 NLT

onathan could not believe his ears. Then again yes, he could—his father, Saul, thought only of himself. He wondered if his father would ever learn the cost of moving by mindless impulse. He spoke without thinking, being careful only to protect himself at the cost of everyone else. Except now the "everyone else" was him. But that mattered not to Saul. His political career came before his children or even the warning of the prophets. He did his own thing, feigning deference to God but fooling no one in the process.

Now, out of ignorance, Jonathan had fallen into the line of his father's fire. Completely unaware of Saul's decree to kill anyone who ate food before evening—before he had avenged himself on his enemies—Jonathan scooped up some honey and ate it. He wondered why the others, who had the lackluster look of hunger and fatigue on their countenances, didn't do likewise. It was then that he heard of the decree, and it made no sense to him. How could hungry men fight effectively? Once again, because of his posturing, Saul had spoken to the detriment of his army. The men, exhausted after fighting the Philistines, fell upon the plunder too exhausted and famished to separate the blood from the meat. Someone pointed out that the men had fallen into sin in their haste to abate their appetites, and so Saul built an altar to the Lord to deter His anger. But was even this a sincere step on his part? No, he simply wanted to be free to return to the battle. The priests, however, recommended that they seek God before confronting the Philistines. This caused Saul great consternation. He was anxious to get on with the war. In haste he called for a lot to be drawn, swearing that if the sin that held them back from victory was upon even his son Jonathan, then he must die. He was willing to sacrifice even his own son for his selfish gain!

Jonathan, against his greater knowledge, still hoped there was something in his father that would click into good sense. Saul, though, was too far down the road to turn back now. It would be too much for him to admit that he was wrong. He had to go through with his decree to save face. Far be it from him to gain the reputation of a pushover, and so he stood his ground. He said it; he must now go through with it. But the men grew indignant. For once they could not go along with Saul's impulsiveness. They thought of themselves. If the life of his own son meant so little to the king, what was the value of their own lives? They were disturbed as they thought of their leader in this context. It was only a matter of time before their lives would be sacrificed without a second thought.

The pattern had grown too familiar, and now it was time to break it. So the men rose to Jonathan's defense.

They defied Saul's orders, reasoning with him that it was Jonathan who had led them to victory; was this to be his reward? If so, they would have no part in it. How could they take the life of one who had saved their own? At this, Saul, forever swayed by the opinion of others, relented. But something inside of Jonathan broke that day and left a void that only God could fill. The tie that binds father and son together had been severed by the cutting words of the father's foolish vow. That his father would sacrifice his son to save face was the worst kind of affront. Jonathan always thought that a father was supposed to make sacrifices for the sake of his children. At least, this was *his* definition of love. But Saul loved only himself. Therefore Jonathan would turn his eyes upon God and give his heart to One more deserving. To One who thought it not robbery to sacrifice for Him.

In what ways have your parents disappointed you? The human frailties of our earthly parents can cause us pain from time to time. They can also do a lot to form our opinions of ourselves and shape our character. Jonathan knew his father had serious flaws, yet he tried his best to honor him in spite of them. This was not always easy. Eventually his close friendship with David gave him the bonding experience he never felt with Saul. David understood relationships and proved to be a steadfast friend. This was an extension of the relationship he had with God. Perhaps David shared with Jonathan what I would like to share with you now. While earthly parents can disappoint, we have a Heavenly Parent who never disappoints us. He is altogether lovely and perfect in every way. No dysfunctions here! When others give us distorted visions of who we are, He is there to affirm us and reveal who He created us to be—fearfully and wonderfully made, totally special, utterly loved and treasured. As a matter of fact, He loves us so much that He sacrificed His Only Son for us. Not out of foolish impulse. Not out of selfishness. But out of complete selflessness for our sakes. His sacrifice was made to forge a bond between us and Him that no outside force could ever sever. Nothing can separate us from His love.

> *Dear Heavenly Father, though I realize that human beings are not perfect, something inside of me expects more from my parents than they are able to give. Their failure to live up to my expectations and fill all of my needs leaves me wounded at times. I struggle often with my own identity in light of this. Even though they are there for me physically, I sometimes feel a deep sense of abandonment within. It is a void that creates great pain. I ask that You come and fill those empty places. That You be my Abba Father. That You pour out the love of a Father on me and heal the scars on my heart and in my mind. That Your presence be my affirmation. I choose to hide myself in You under the protection of Your wings, and rest in Your parentage. In Jesus' name, amen.*

Maddening Times

After this time had passed, I, Nebuchadnezzar, looked up to heaven. My sanity returned, and I praised and worshiped the Most High and honored the one who lives forever.

DANIEL 4:34 NLT

"Ah, this is the life..." Nebuchadnezzar stretched beneath the finery of his robes, feeling the silk caress his skin as the breeze atop his palatial rooftop perch cooled his bronzed cheeks. Yes, this was the life, and he had created it with his own hands. As far as the eye could see—as a matter of fact, even that which you couldn't see—it all belonged to him. What treasures he had accumulated! Among his favorites were the gold and silver vessels taken from the temple in Jerusalem. And then there was the majestic gold statue he had created. He frowned slightly as he recalled the controversy that had ensued after those three Hebrew boys refused to bow and worship it. They did indeed serve a powerful God. Why, after he had them thrown into the fiery furnace as punishment for their obstinance, this same God had descended from the heavenlies to walk in the midst of the flames with them. He had not even allowed the smell of smoke to penetrate their garments! No wonder they were so passionate in their allegiance to Him.

But none of the gods that Nebuchadnezzar acknowledged had ever displayed this same sort of intimate relationship with their worshipers, so he chose to remain cerebral in his approach to this "religion thing." He decided that if you didn't mess with the gods, they didn't mess with you. But what of the God of Daniel, Shadrach, Meshach, and Abednego? He had shown Himself mighty on their behalf, and the king had been forced to acknowledge His greatness. But what if it was all smoke and lights? Nebuchadnezzar knew that the magicians and sorcerers in his own court were capable of performing absolutely amazing tricks that could easily persuade one to conclude that they were assisted by a fearsome and mysterious god. Oh, well, whatever worked for them. As for himself, he believed firmly that the gods help those who help themselves. And he had helped himself rather well. He had built this kingdom with his own sweat and tears, his own brilliant military strategies, his own dreams—without any supernatural intervention.

And so Nebuchadnezzar ignored Daniel's warning of what would happen if he didn't acknowledge that "the Most High rules over the kingdoms of the world and gives them to anyone He chooses." The king chose to cling to his own personal brand of belief, the one that made him now sigh with great satisfaction as he surveyed the expanse of territory he reigned over. "Just look at this great city of Babylon!" he boasted. "I, *by my own mighty power,* have built this beautiful city as my royal residence and as an expression of *my* royal splendor." And on that note, he teetered on the brink of God's displeasure, then fell into the abyss of the deepest darkness a mortal could experience. For God had resisted his pride and removed the mantle of His favor, and there was nothing left once He withdrew. Not even the ability to maintain a sound mind. And so this great and powerful "self-made" king was reduced to wandering alone...driven from human society, living in the fields with the wild animals, eating grass like a common cow for seven years until something in his inner man broke and he yielded to the knowledge that, yes, there was One greater than himself...One who gave the power to gain wealth.

What rewards or accolades have you taken for yourself? If we're not careful, we, too, can become drunk with our own sense of power. We develop convenient amnesia about the grace and giftings of God. We prefer to laud what we perceive as our own accomplishments won by our own efforts. But this thinking is madness. How, then, could we explain two people of equal intelligence and talents leading two very different existences? One of prosperity, one of mediocrity. Or one who is unqualified being exalted? The deciding factor becomes not the ingenuity of men, but solely the favor of God. Favor is merely One superior bending in the direction of one who is knowingly inferior. Without the favor of God, we are left to wander alone in the dark, in the wilderness of our own lack of understanding—keeping company with those who are no more than animals, free of a conscience that fears God, eating grass, experiencing that which is lower than what God intended for our spirit's consumption, preferring the counsel of the ungodly over the King's bread. The King's bread, God's Word, is the source of our life. And we, like Nebuchadnezzar, inevitably deteriorate—spiritually, physically, and emotionally—until we come to our senses and realize that pride is a lonely country that harbors no desirable citizens.

And so Nebuchadnezzar looked up to heaven. His sanity returned, and he praised and worshiped the Most High and honored the One who lives forever. And when his sanity returned, so did his honor and glory and kingdom. He was reestablished as head of his domain with even greater honor than before. But not before he learned one extremely vital lesson: It is a dangerous thing to praise yourself and ignore the One who made you. God refuses to share His glory with another—and that includes you. It is only when we truly make Jesus Lord of our lives that He makes us lord over all that lies within our reach, and even more.

Dear Heavenly Father, in a world where we are pro-grammed to make things happen, help me to always remember that You are the true author of days and accomplishments. Help me to walk circumspectly before You, redeeming the time, recognizing every season, never leaning to my own understanding, but totally trusting in You. Help me, in the midst of every victory, to seek Your purpose and agenda. Help me to work with diligence, always knowing that You are the start and end of all that I do. Let me never pre-sume to share Your glory. But rather let men see my good works and glorify You in Heaven. But most of all, dear God, Abba Father, let me bring a smile to Your heart as I lay all of my trophies before You. In Jesus' name, amen.

Wrenching Times

*Then the Lord said to me, "Go and get
your wife again. Bring her back to you and
love her, even though she loves adultery."*

HOSEA 3:1 NLT

*H*osea knew what they were saying as he
walked down the street, his head hung low in pain. Their
conversations bore into his back along with their eyes.
Some cast glances of pity, others of incredulity that he
could be such a fool. Some were obviously past the point
of sympathy, so great was their disgust that he would
allow his wife to continue to behave in the way that she
did. *Why should Hosea put up with Gomer's adulterous
ways?* they wondered. Surely the law gave him compensation for a wife who insisted upon being wayward. But
though Hosea knew all of this, he persisted in his love for
Gomer.

The people shook their heads and wagged their
tongues, watching him run after her as she left him time
and time again to follow her lovers. And when her suitors

were cold and cruel to her, stripping her of all she had, Hosea would faithfully make sure that Gomer had sufficient food and drink. He even provided her with linen and jewelry, which she took and either offered to Baal or shared with her various men. How much of an imbecile could Hosea be? Even the parentage of the children she bore was in question. How could Hosea be sure they were his own in the midst of her wanderings? She only returned when she came to herself and realized she would be better off with Hosea. But this decision lasted only for a season before her spirit grew restless. Hosea could see the boredom and the wanderlust begin to fill her eyes. He would silently pray for her to remain with him, but he would return home after a day of business to find her gone once again. The rumor mill was always faithful to supply her location. And Hosea, knowing the man she was currently with had nothing to offer, would leave provisions for her and go his way patiently awaiting her return.

Yes, it was true Hosea's pain was great—but Hosea was a prophet. His life was a parable come to life that showed how God felt about the children of Israel. He was the faithful husband longing after his unfaithful wife. Always willing to forgive, to comfort and restore, regardless of the offense. And so Hosea continued on his trek to find Gomer and look after her welfare. He found her this time broken and in even deeper trouble than the last time he'd rescued her from one of her paramours. This time she had been sold into slavery. No one could believe that he would spend even one shekel to buy her back, yet that was exactly what he did. With fifteen shekels of silver and about a homer and a lethek of barley, he bought her back and took her home, speaking tenderly to her all the way while she looked on with unappreciative eyes.

Hosea didn't mind doing this for his wife; he knew that everyone was given a season of grace before judgment would come. God would not forsake him and allow him to be abused forever. He would come with deliverance in His wings and restoration in His hands. Until then Hosea would wait on the Lord, allowing Him to renew his strength. For he had been party to the fellowship of God's suffering with His people. If anyone knew His heart at this point, it was Hosea. He knew the pain of separation and unfaithfulness and how, in spite of it all, love prevailed. It was strange to describe this thing called love or figure out exactly how it worked. It was higher than he imagined, yet bent lower than he thought he would ever be able to go. And yet it expanded beyond the widest reaches of his soul, even when offended by the object of his affection. It was certainly larger than him, Hosea concluded, yet it included him completely in the circle of God's endless love. It was that love that freed Hosea to love the "unlovable."

What can separate us from the love of God? Our own foolishness? Mindless mistakes? Deceived hearts or distorted vision? No, nothing can stop Him from longing after us, from being willing to forgive us time and time again. This does not, however, separate us from the consequences of our sin. Nevertheless, He is there, ready to heal the sting that consequences bring until we finally learn that it is not profitable to stray. But in the meantime His agape love, that "in spite of yourself" love, covers a multitude of sins. Its wooing power takes us to another place of humble surrender. For who can resist a lover who gives all, even when we're not ready to receive? It's simply a matter of time before we find ourselves addicted to His goodness. Completely "soul'd" out, finding all other influences who come to woo us hopelessly inferior to Him.

Dear Heavenly Father, forgive me for the times I've strayed and gone in search of the other lovers of my soul. Forgive me for the times I gave in to those who courted my flesh and abused the deposit of Your Spirit within me. As I return to You, I pray that You will wash my heart and make my spirit new within me. Cast me not away from Your presence, my Lord and Savior. I, like David, cry out, "Take not Your Holy Spirit from me." Restore the joy of my salvation to assuage the sting of sin. As You surround me once again with Your love, do not allow the shouts of condemnation to drown out Your tender voice. Speak to me and I will listen and yield to what You say. Hedge me in round about and keep me by Your side. And as I learn of Your bountiful grace and mercy, help me to rest in Your peace, safe within Your arms forevermore. In Jesus' name, amen.

Urgent Times

*Just then a woman who had been subject to bleeding
for twelve years came up behind him and touched
the edge of his cloak. She said to herself,
If I only touch his cloak, I will be healed.*

Matthew 9:20,21

She had nothing to lose, for everything had been lost already. She had spent all she had on physicians who offered a cure yet never delivered. Her health had been spent along with her money. Weak and anemic from bleeding for so many years, she saw this Jesus as her last resort. The stigma of being continually unclean was too much for her to bear. But on this day she had no concern for the jostling crowd and those who pressed against her; she was on a mission.

After all that she had heard concerning Jesus, she had purposed in her heart that she must get to Him. And so she had waited for His arrival. It was Jesus or nothing. Clasping her hope against her breast with bony fingers, she decided that perhaps she should not ask Him to touch her. She could not bear His refusal. It stood to reason that she was of small consequence in light of the more urgent matters of others. No, she wouldn't bother Him with her issue. If He was all that she had heard, she believed that there would be healing power even in His garments. She reasoned within herself that if what flowed from within her had the power to make anything she sat or lay upon unclean, and anyone who touched where she had been became unclean as well, then surely the virtue that flowed within this man was also on whatever He touched, including His clothing. "If I just touch His cloak, I will be made whole," she said to herself. If there was a penalty to pay, it would be worth it, so great was her longing to be made whole.

It was now or never—she instinctively knew this. So as the pressing of the crowd grew more insistent, she stretched forth her hand and touched the edge of His cloak. Time stood still in suspended animation. Strength began to course through her limbs, and she could feel the flow of blood stopping. She had been made whole! But her rejoicing was cut short as Jesus stopped abruptly. The crowd also stopped. His voice was magnified over the silence: "Who touched Me?" The people looked from one to the other, hunching their shoulders, looking vaguely perplexed. Touched Him? How could He not be touched in the middle of such a throng? Everyone was touching Him, but certainly not deliberately. They were not here to offend; they had come simply to see Him. To get a word, to get a touch as He willingly chose to do so. No, indeed, no one had touched Him on purpose. And why would this be an occurrence of note anyway? But He continued to insist that someone had touched Him. He had felt virtue leave His body. In that instant she knew that she was the culprit and that she dare not hide. She could not steal her healing. She only prayed that when she confessed, it would not be taken from her.

Pressing forward, head held low, knees trembling, she could no longer stand in His presence. Falling at His feet, she poured out her story to Him. Of the pain, the shame, the suffering she had endured. How she hadn't wanted to bother Him. But she was desperate. She just wanted to be well again. To be made whole. To have a normal life. Surely He could understand her distress and have pity.... And then true healing came! He released her to go in peace, acknowledging her faith. "Her faith had made her whole," He said. Oh, if only she had believed sooner...but today was just as good a day to begin.

What are the things that you feel hinder you from being whole? To accept the labels that life puts on us is to accept certain defeat. It is up to us to press through the crowd of doubts, fears, and untruths that keep us bound. Stretching forth and breaking through to the place where we reach Jesus and grab hold of His virtue must become our all-consuming mission. By exercising our arms of faith, we strengthen our whole body. We must stop allowing the enemy to drain us with negative confessions about ourselves. We are not doomed to forever live in defeat. We are not lost causes. We are desirable. We are lovable. We are wanted. We have all that we need within us because Jesus lives inside of us. In our weakness He is made strong. Let God arise within you. Let Him empower you to receive the healing—mental, spiritual, emotional, or physical—that is already yours to embrace.

> *Dear Heavenly Father, I realize that in and of myself*
> *I can do nothing and that I am nothing without You.*
> *I celebrate my nothingness, realizing that in this I*
> *leave room for You to be everything in me—all the*

strength I need. All the power I need. All the love I need. I am complete in You, for You are my sufficiency. Thank You for Your constant care and compassion. Thank You for meeting me where I am today. In the midst of all my fears and turmoil, make Yourself available for another touch. Another touch to renew my faith and rebuild the broken areas of my spirit. As I reach out to You, meet me with all that I need to overcome my present trials as well as those things that seek to cling from my past. In Jesus' name, amen.

In striving to find You I trip over myself
and my stinging flesh distracts me from Your love
In straining to hear You
my questions drown out Your answers
and I accuse You of not listening
In grasping to receive Your blessing
my hands get in the way
and I drop Your promises...
but then You lovingly stoop
and recover them
far more patient with me than I am with myself
You wait for me
to come to the end of myself
and the beginning of You....

Remorseful Times

Then Peter remembered the word Jesus had spoken,
"Before the rooster crows, you will disown me three times."
And he went outside and wept bitterly.

MATTHEW 26:75

What is it about my mouth? Peter wondered. It seemed to have a life all its own. It didn't matter what he intended to do in his heart; his mouth ignored his good intentions and took off on an entirely different course. *Why do I do that?* he wondered. He was invariably saying something he shouldn't say, and Jesus was continually rebuking him. It always seemed the right thing to say until the words came out of his mouth. They then turned sour and left a bitter feeling in the pit of his stomach. Peter remembered the countless times that Jesus had questioned the motive of his heart based on the things he had said. And each question magnified his lack of understanding concerning God's purposes in Jesus' life. Peter thought he got it, but he really didn't. He realized that now more than ever since Jesus had been arrested. He felt confused, thrown off balance, afraid, no—downright terrified. Every-thing had happened around him way too fast. He felt as if he were one pebble in the midst of a huge avalanche and he was forced either to roll in the rush down the mountain or be crushed. And so his mouth had once again spouted words in haste—words that never should have been spoken. Except this time the words were more offensive than any he had ever uttered before.

Jesus had told Peter that he would deny Him three times before the cock crowed. Peter had thought it quite insulting at the time. *How could He ever think I would do such a thing? Doesn't He know how much I love Him?* he had thought. Jesus' words had hurt him deeply. What did He take him for? And why have Peter around if He thought so little of him? He felt that he was being judged for his impulsiveness, which had become an obvious trait in Peter's life. He felt weary at the thought. Would he ever be able to live down his reputation for always saying the wrong thing at the wrong time? Well, this time he had really done it. He had denied Jesus—three times before the cock crowed, just like He said it would happen. But this time it was not just a matter of realizing he had said something he shouldn't have. Peter felt it sealed Jesus' fate in a strange sort of way. If this had come to pass, it meant that all the other things Jesus had said would come to pass, too.

Why had he denied Jesus? Was it because he feared being recognized as the one who had cut off the soldier's ear in the garden? Was he afraid of being accused of treason against the Roman government and suffering some brutal punishment? What had happened to Peter's declarations of being willing to die with Jesus? Those had quickly gone out the window when his own skin was being threatened. What a wimp! And Jesus had known all along exactly what he had been made of. The truth hurt, and Peter wept bitterly. He wept over all the lost opportunities to do something that really counted. The conversations that were never truly appreciated. The words he never took to heart. The revelations he refused to embrace. The truth he refused to see. And now the time was gone. Jesus was gone. He would never have another chance to show Him how far he had come. And he had contributed to his beloved Teacher's demise. Why had Jesus ever called Peter to follow Him if He knew all of his weaknesses? What had He seen in him that was worth salvaging? And now that he'd blown it, where could he go to get away from himself and what he had done? Where could he go for forgiveness? For restoration?

Oh, would there be no end to his weeping and brokenness of heart? Days of emptiness passed while Peter rehearsed his regrets over and over again. And then Mary came, saying that Jesus had risen from the dead! Did he dare hope for another chance to make amends? But when Jesus appeared to him, He never addressed Peter's denial. Never accused or rebuked him for his weakness. He had moved beyond yesterday. His mind was on the future. "Peter, do you love me?" What a question! Of course he loved Jesus! "Then feed my sheep," his Teacher answered. It was the least Peter could do. No longer did he feel any fear and trembling or false bravado. There was something he wanted more than the acceptance of men, something he never wanted to be separated from again—the love of his Lord. The impulsive little boy in Peter had died with Jesus on the cross, and a man had been resurrected with his Savior. Though he had denied Him in the face of a small cluster, he would now go to the ends of the world to proclaim the Name of Jesus. Gone were his insecurities. Gone was his fear of repercussions or even of death. Peter knew now what he did not know before—nothing could separate him from God's love.

What are some of the past failings in your life that you have found difficult to get over? These failings can speak with cruel voices that accuse and demoralize us. They tell us that we are no longer worthy of God's love and attention. That we've messed up big time. That there is no redemption of our circumstance. Our self-worth plummets, and we begin to agree with our accuser that there is nothing good in us, nothing worth salvaging. And then Jesus comes with a new commission for our lives, heaping blessings on top of our incredulity that He still loves us in spite of our foolishness. He extends His grace to us for a new beginning and a better tomorrow, and we're made a little stronger and a whole lot wiser. Thank God for His mercy, for He knows we are but dust. Thank God that He is the God of as many chances as we need to get it right!

> *Dear Heavenly Father, I thank You. I thank You*
> *simply because You have chosen to love me. In spite*
> *of my failings and my flaws, You continue to extend*
> *Your mercy and grace to me. Without it I am*
> *nothing, but with it I am filled with the sufficiency of*
> *all that I need to become all that You would have*
> *me to be. I stand before You as a willing vessel*
> *longing to pour out to others all that You have*
> *deposited in me. Fill me with Your understanding*
> *and wisdom that I might walk in the Spirit and not*
> *be drawn away by the rationalizations of the flesh.*
> *Replace my fears with unshakable faith that I might*
> *forsake the opinions of man and strive to please only*
> *You. Fill me with a love and passion for You that*
> *overrides my appetite for anything that is not of You.*
> *Help me to exercise discipline and walk in agreement*
> *with You as You order my steps, my words, and my*
> *thoughts. Let all that I do be found acceptable in*
> *Your sight. In Jesus' name, amen.*

Perhaps I thought I had to reach too high to get to You
who knows the excuse?
it always seems too easy
to simply find You
where You always are
waiting for me…
for who is man
that God should desire him
live for him
die for him?
and yet You've done just that
and I am ashamed of my own selfishness
my own insistence that You be complicated
giving me a reason to admire
my own spirituality
it is far too humbling to know
that all I have to do
is call Your name.…

Reaching Times

He wanted to see who Jesus was, but being
a short man he could not, because of the crowd.

LUKE 19:3

Ignoring those who glared openly at him as he passed by, Zacchaeus kept his eyes focused on the object of his concentration. He didn't care that they hated him. He didn't care that they resented his presence. He had one mission in mind—seeing this man who everyone was talking about. This Jesus. From his vantage point he strained to see Him. The crowd seemed to block his view on purpose, milling about their enigmatic guest. Not one to be put off easily, Zacchaeus determined to devise a way to see Him. Who was this Jesus? Another religious zealot who would incite the people not to pay their taxes? This could cause great problems for him. He had to scope this guy out—get a handle on him, and plan his next move accordingly. Yes, he must see this Jesus if it was the last thing he did. So let the people think whatever they wanted to think; their stares would not deter him.

Running ahead of the throng, Zacchaeus scoped out the scenery for the perfect spot. Aha! Perfect! This tree would serve as an excellent vantage point for him. So up he climbed, finding the perfect view on one of the lower branches. He could actually witness everything he needed to see and hear without being noticed, far removed from the press of the crowd. But all of a sudden Jesus looked up, straight into his eyes. He froze, not knowing what to expect. Would Jesus now resort to hurling accusations at him? He would be an easy target. Everyone hated him. He was wealthy, a tax collector, and they accused him of being a traitor and a cheat. Yes, he would be the perfect scapegoat if that's what Jesus needed to manipulate the crowd into seeing things His way. But instead Jesus did something entirely unexpected. He asked Zacchaeus to come down from his lofty seat and take Him to his house. Just think—this Jesus wanted to be his houseguest! Who would have thought it?

This did not set well with the crowd at all. Immediately a wave of disapproval swept through the gathering, but Jesus seemed oblivious as He focused on Zacchaeus. Zacchaeus, on the other hand, was so thrown off-balance by this strange invitation that he was initially taken aback. And then it hit him. Jesus was sincere! He really *did* want to get to know him. *Little ol' me,* Zacchaeus thought. *I am the one that everyone despises and yet their hero wants to spend time with me,* Zacchaeus thought. This had a strange effect on him. It was humbling to be sincerely reached out to. No one had extended this sort of kindness to him for as long as he could remember.

From the time he was a child, he had been ridiculed because of his small stature. Pushed and shoved. Teased and tormented. Many a tear of self-pity had been shed.

Deep within his childlike heart Zacchaeus vowed that things would be notably different when he grew up. No one would push him around—he would be the one calling the shots. And those who made his life difficult would get a taste of their own medicine. He would show them all. And so he took advantage of the system instilled by the Romans and moved up the ranks to become a tax collector. He had not cared about the people who struggled to keep up with what they owed. He showed no mercy when demanding balances from his debtors. The taunts of the neighborhood children came back to haunt him, and those were enough to strengthen his resolve. He would not back down.

And now Jesus didn't care about his size. Didn't care that he was a tax collector. Didn't care that He would receive bad press because he chose to associate with Zacchaeus. Suddenly Zacchaeus felt important—not because of position, not because the Roman government said so or because the people said so. He felt important because *God* said so. As affirmation flooded his heart, his mind was changed, his countenance transformed. Suddenly he saw himself for what he had become. Saw how his striving to be over people had actually belittled him even beneath his diminutive stature. He wanted to be totally deserving of God's compassion. Though that could never be, he had to do something as a token of gratitude. It was interesting what a word from God could do. Suddenly all that he had hoarded in order to build himself up meant nothing. A word from God had made him full. "Look, Lord," he vowed, "here and now I give half of my possessions to the poor, and if I have cheated anybody out of anything, I will pay him back four times the amount." The relief he felt upon uttering this promise was like opening wellsprings deep within his soul. Joy washed over him like a waterfall. He was free! Free to be accepted! Free to be loved! Free to be embraced as a son of God! For the first time, Zacchaeus knew what it was like to truly stand tall.

> *The beauty we can find in the midst of*
> *our own imagined failings is that God*
> *loves us just the way we are.*

What are the things about yourself that you don't like? Short-comings truly do cause us to "act out," to overcompensate for the me we think we should be. Trying to measure up to the standards of others can be debilitating because we will undoubtedly fall short of their expectations. The beauty we can find in the midst of our own imagined failings is that God loves us just the way we are. He doesn't think we're too tall, too short, too fat, too thin, too dark, too light, too ugly, or too anything. He just sees His child struggling for affirmation, for the reassurance that we're all right. And based on our relationship with Him, He gently reminds us that we are fearfully and wonderfully made. Deliberately crafted just the way we are to be a unique member of His divine family. One that He welcomes with open arms because all of our imperfections become perfect in the light of His love.

Dear Heavenly Father, I apologize for the times I
have looked in the mirror and failed to see what You
see. I pray that my lack of appreciation has not been

*an insult to Your handiwork. Open my eyes to see
my beauty in the light of Your love. Grant me an
appreciation of the me that You've created and help
me to give it all back to You for the fulfillment of
Your purposes. I choose to walk in the beauty of holiness when my flesh tugs me toward the ugliness of
sin. May my stature be measured by my righteousness and not by physical inches. Today I release the
disappointment I have felt over what I feel I should
have been and lay all that I am and all that I hope
to be at Your feet. Renew my mind so that I may get
a new vision of what is truly important. Take me
and make me an instrument of Your love and
power. In Jesus' name, amen.*

Resigning Times

*"...but we had hoped that he was the one who was
going to redeem Israel. And what is more, it is
the third day since all this took place. In addition,
some of our women amazed us. They went to the tomb
early this morning but didn't find his body."*

LUKE 24:21

Sadness hung like a heavy, wet blanket over the
men as they walked. Completely lost in thought, they continued commiserating amongst themselves on the events
of days gone by, unable to shake the disappointment and
depression they felt at Jesus' departure from their midst.
Jesus was gone. They had hoped that He was the Messiah,
but once again their hopes had been dashed. And now He
was gone. Even more perplexing, the women in the group
had returned from His gravesite to say that His body was
missing. Yes, some of the disciples swore that they had
seen an angel, who told them that Jesus had risen from the
dead. Yet how were they supposed to believe that? Considering the treachery of what had recently taken place, it
seemed quite clear that His body had been stolen. Who
would put it past those men who had been bent on

causing trouble and stirring the masses against Jesus? Couldn't they have just granted Him the peace of leaving His body in the grave? Was that too much to ask? It was hard enough to absorb all that had occurred without this new and traumatic turn of events.

As they walked and talked, Jesus joined them. But so deep was their sorrow they did not recognize Him. The tears in their soul distorted their vision, and He became just another stranger to them. And then this stranger had the audacity to interrupt their conversation. He asked them what things had them so deeply concerned. What things? *What things!* Where had this man come from? Hadn't He heard any news of the last four days? He simply stood there, calmly taking them in, His face free from pain or worry while they were practically bowed over with their cares. Now they must stand and explain to this clueless stranger the things that grieved their very souls. And then He called them foolish! They didn't know if they should grow indignant or just ignore Him as He began to quote scripture after scripture of the prophets' predictions about the Messiah. Though they failed to see how this connected to what they had told Him, it comforted them in a strange way. And so they invited their new companion to remain with them for the evening.

As they sat to eat, they felt as if they were experiencing déjà vu. Their guest took the bread, broke it and blessed it, and suddenly their eyes were open. But as soon as they recognized Him, He had vanished. *But of course!* they thought. They should have known! They recalled the way they had felt when He began to unfold the scriptures to them as they walked. How could they have been so blind? They must tell the others! They would not make the same mistake again if given another opportunity to see Him. By the time they reached the other disciples, Peter too had seen Him. It was all too much for them to take in. How

could this be? Was He a figment of their imagination, perhaps their own wishful thinking had willed Him back to
them in the form of a mirage? And then He was standing
among them again. And they were afraid. As He ate the
food they provided, He fed them with more heavenly
fare—bread from the Word of God. Finally they understood all that He had tried to reveal to them before. What
was formerly dead to them became alive in their hearts,
and the truth rang in their spirits. This time as Jesus was
taken away on a cloud into glory, His absence had an
entirely different effect on His disciples. Instead of being
defeated by depression, they were invigorated with joy.
Despair was replaced by faith while loss was eradicated
by restoration. They had a hope, a future, an expected
end. And a profound message to share with the world!

Do you need a little perspective on a loss in your life? "Every
good-bye ain't gone," the old folks say. And it is true. The things that
we think are dead in our lives miraculously return anew when the
Lord breathes on them. As we bemoan the fate of lost dreams, lost
loves, and lost opportunities, Jesus sidles up beside us. As we mourn
the loss of what once filled us with hope or fulfillment, He asks us,
"What things?" Sometimes in the depth of our despair, we also don't
recognize His visitation. We spend far more time grieving than we
ought to and miss the opportunity to rejoice with the One who has
control over all "things" in our lives. When we finally get to the place
where we understand that nothing is lost in Him, and that everything
that is of God in our lives will always remain, life will become a more
even road to travel. When we look to see Jesus walking beside us,
then, and only then, will we be able to embrace the power and help
He brings to restore all we feel we've lost.

Dear Heavenly Father, I take all that I've seemingly lost and all that I hope to gain and place them on Your altar. I know that it is not by might, not by power, but by Your Spirit that all things are gained. I know also that You are able to keep whatever is committed to You. So with that in mind, I commit all my dreams, hopes, desires, and longings into Your hands. Please keep them safe and deliver them up at the right time. I know that You know what is best for me and that You know the way I take. So I ask for the deliverance of Your perfect plan for me according to Your divine timetable. Help me to remember that nothing is lost in You and all that I am is found only in You. In Jesus' name, amen.

Passive Times

*"Sir," the invalid replied, "I have no one to help me into
the pool when the water is stirred. While I am trying
to get in, someone else goes down ahead of me."*

JOHN 5:7

For a long time He watched the man lying
among the rest of the afflicted. Resignation had etched
permanent lines into his face, making him look old
beyond his years. Thirty-eight years had come and gone
and nothing had changed in his life but the date. His condition remained the same. Unable to move, he was con-
fined to his mat, to whatever spot he landed in until
someone kind enough moved him to another locale. As
Jesus watched him, knowing all the history of this man's
pain, He waited until the invalid's eye caught His. He
questioned his desire to be made whole. The man on the
rug thought his condition was evident. Why would this
man ask such a question? Couldn't He see that he was too
far away from the pool? By the time he made it almost
close enough to get in, someone else would beat him into

the pool. He couldn't help it. He was a slave to his inability. And now this stranger had the nerve to ask him if he would be made whole. How could he be when he had no man to put him into the pool?

How could He tell him to pick up his mat and walk? How could He make it sound so simple? If it had been that simple, he would have done it a long time ago. Just get up and walk? Just like that? Who was this man? And why should he believe Him? What made this man think he, a cripple, was in the habit of heeding the advice of perfect strangers? Yet after thirty-eight years what would it cost him to simply believe? Something about the demeanor of this man caused the invalid to take Him at His word, to dare to believe that if he followed His instruction he would not be disappointed. Over the years many had experimented, offering this antidote or that formula to no avail. He had grown weary of all the suggestions and resigned to the pool of Bethesda as a last resort. It was said that an angel came and stirred the waters, and that if you could get in the current you would be miraculously healed. This he had witnessed. Though some might say he was grasping at straws, the pool was his last shot. But sitting on the porch had wearied him. He had grown more disillusioned with every passing day. Others passed him by, shoving their way in, oblivious of others, as they desperately sought their own miracles. And he, no longer possessing the strength to even attempt to reach the water's edge, looked on, growing more apathetic as others received and he did not.

And now here was this mysterious man telling him to rise as easily as if He were saying that the sky was blue. Why was it that people who were not subject to suffering could so glibly tell others what to do about their condition? All of these things went through his head as he looked into the calm countenance of the man. Perhaps He did care on some level. At least He had stopped to speak to him, which was more than most did. They merely wandered through, stepping over the sick as if they had been left there to rot. Yes, this stranger was different. And something in His eyes gave the invalid the courage to defy the odds of his own thinking, to risk failure and rise from his pallet. Leaping to his feet, he folded his pallet and began to walk.

Glory be to God! He walked! What had he been waiting for all these years? Jehovah be praised! Surely he had been visited by redemption. The grace of God had touched him this day. It was truly a miracle! To think that he had accepted his fate for so many years; it now seemed nonsensical. His faith had made him whole. Why hadn't he believed sooner? He turned to ask Jesus these questions and more, but He had vanished. How phenomenal the difference a few moments with this peculiar man had made. His life was irrevocably changed. All that he had attempted to achieve in his own human efforts had come to pass by a few words from this man who had disappeared. This man whose face would be indelibly imprinted on his heart forever.

Healing is a touchy subject. Why are some healed and others are not? Stories of those determined to get what God promised and take His word at face value bear evidence that He will not deny those who draw upon His anointing for their deliverance. Many of us stand or sit so close to our deliverance but have grown weary in the struggle. We yield to the temptation to stop inches short of the blessing. Like a woman in labor nearing the time of her delivery, we need the strength to give one last push. And then Jesus arrives on the scene and tells us to simply rise, calling on what He has placed within us to overcome. His words of assurance bring renewed strength. His words remove the weight from our shoulders and place it on His. It is His Word that is on the line. And He cannot lie. As we follow His direction, He manifests His promises to us and sets us free to believe, free to be healed.

> *Dear Heavenly Father, my faith has been exhausted as I have struggled in my own strength to overcome the situations in my life that wound and paralyze me. I call upon You to visit me and renew my strength. Grant me a word that will become life in my inner man and make me whole. Help my unbelief. I reach out to You to help me rise from the dust of my own resignation and begin again. I choose to believe You. I choose to take You at Your Word. I choose to follow You now, today. I will no longer dwell on past experiences and failures. I decisively yield my life to You, expecting a change for the better as I obey Your Word. In Jesus' name, amen.*

You will never leave me or forsake me
these words sound strangely familiar
said by far too many
who didn't keep their promise
yet for every time I think You gone
I find You nearer than I thought
sometimes invisible from my denial
unrecognizably marred by my unbelief
silent in the face of my raging anger
immovable in spite of my momentary rejections
You are still there
constantly there
never turning
never changing
casting no shadows
to the left or right
You continue standing
firmly rooted
in the center of Your promise
"I will never leave you or forsake you…"
from Your lips
to my heart….

Repentant Times

Then Mary took about a pint of pure nard,
an expensive perfume; she poured it on Jesus' feet
and wiped his feet with her hair. And the house
was filled with the fragrance of the perfume.

JOHN 12:3

What could Mary give him? He had given her so much. Anything she set before Him would seem paltry. Yet her heart burned to give Him some token, some expression of her love. This was not an ordinary man. What pleased others would not necessarily have the same effect on Him. She knew somehow that the usual womanly shows of affection would be inappropriate, yet she longed to show Him her heart. Don't be mistaken—this was not a matter of physical attraction or even romantic longing. This was something deeper. The effect He had on her was different from any other encounter she had ever experienced with members of the opposite sex.

His eyes seemed to see down to the bottom of her soul. She almost felt naked under His gaze, yet she did not feel ashamed. Instead she felt strangely consoled that He saw all but did not judge or belittle her. Rather, He seemed to understand and offer her a greater measure of compassion and caring because of the knowing. Since meeting Him, Mary did not feel alone in her secrets. This could be unsettling yet comforting at the same time. When He spoke, His words were deep and profound, separating her soul from her spirit. His words renewed her mind and transformed her life. She was not the woman she had been. No, meeting Him had changed her forever. His very presence had a strangely calming effect. She found herself looking at things more soberly, looking beneath the surface of what her eyes saw. Yes, Jesus had changed Mary. Matured her. Revealed to her who she really was.

It was in this newfound maturity that a sense of discerning had been unearthed in her. She had not decided if this was a gift she really welcomed, because sometimes it tended to reveal things to her that were not always pleasant. And so this evening, as everyone else reveled in Jesus' visit, Mary felt a little sad. She had a sense that this moment was truly one to be treasured. That no word He spoke should be taken for granted. That every event should be copiously recorded for future posterity. She knew that He would not be with them always. Instinctively, she knew it. Not wanting to embrace this information, it was still a fact she could not shake. He would be leaving them. She didn't know when. She didn't know how. For this reason her gift should be even more precious. It must be something He would never forget. Something that would help her to release Him, because she had given Him her best. In that Mary could rest in comfort once He was gone.

For her this sacrifice was still not enough, but it was all that she had. Worth a year's wages, this precious ointment would be preparation for His departure. It seemed the perfect metaphor for His life, for with every visit, the essence of Him lingered like heavy perfume in the air long after He was gone. And so as she poured all she had on His feet, Mary offered Him all she had. Her worship. In complete submission and servitude she wiped His feet with her hair, deeming any other material far too impersonal. She wanted to pour herself out completely and she saw this as the best way. As the scent rose and filled the house, so did the calm assurance that she could face uncertain days because she had given herself completely to the only One who could insure her future. It didn't matter that others did not understand, only that He understood and accepted her offering in the spirit it had been given. He was pleased with her. He knew her completely. And for Mary that was enough—more than enough, in fact.

When was the last time you let God know in a tangible way how much you really love him? In and of ourselves, what we have to offer the Lord could never be enough to equal the matchless gift He has given to us—His very own life. We find ourselves like the little drummer boy wondering what gift we have that's fit to give the king. The answer seems almost too simple—our worship. God delights to dwell in the midst of our praise. And that praise extends beyond lip service to our submission in obedience to Him. We, too, can bow before His feet in total submission to His Word. It is the purest form of worship that we can offer Him. In this He is always well pleased.

Heavenly Father, I don't hold much in my hands,
but what I have I give to You. Willingly, sparing
nothing, I pour myself out before You. I pray that my

sacrifice of praise and obedience would be a sweet-smelling fragrance. That it would bring pleasure to Your heart. Instruct me in the way that I should take to bring pleasure to Your heart. Help me to maintain a spirit that heeds Your Word without hesitation. I want to be always ready to do Your bidding and be all that You long for me to be. I yield now to You. As my Abba Father. My Lord and King. My Comforter. My Deliverer. My Friend and the Lover of my Soul. I acknowledge all the ways You fill my life with Yourself and ask that You teach me to be a reciprocal gift of all that You have poured out to me. In Jesus' name, amen.

Doubting Times

*Then he said to Thomas, "Put your finger here; see my hands.
Reach out your hand and put it into my side. Stop doubting
and believe." Thomas said to him, "My Lord and my God!"*

JOHN 20:27,28

Thomas looked at them with a mixture of impatience and pity. He understood how they were feeling. The trauma of the past few days had left them all emotionally overwrought. He didn't think that one among them had not pleaded with God to take the day before the crucifixion back, to be able to start all over again and do things differently. In retrospect they had all behaved badly. Scattering to and fro, abandoning Jesus, and leaving Him to fend for Himself in the midst of a hostile crowd. They all knew that liars had been planted to insure His death, but none of them had come forward in His defense. They had all gone underground to save their own skins. This was a bad decision, and they would live with it for the rest of their lives. But was this enough to send them over the edge into the abyss of denial? He felt it highly inappropriate for them to manipulate his emotions this way, telling him that Jesus had risen from the dead, that they had seen Him. How could this be? The man was dead. They all knew that. No, this was going too far. He would not be among the ones who now spread this propaganda and opened themselves up to further ridicule from the enemies of Christ.

In this instance seeing was believing. Thomas would not get caught up in their emotional tirade without proof. Where was Jesus *now* if they had seen Him? Why wasn't He with them? Hadn't they all stayed together before? Surely He would not be out walking among His enemies, would He? But perhaps, after their behavior, they were His enemies as well. Had they stopped to consider that this could be an impostor trying to stir up more trouble for them? No, unless Thomas touched the wounds of Jesus Himself, he would not believe it. And then suddenly Jesus was there as if He had overheard his conversation. After He greeted everyone, He directed His attention toward Thomas. "Put your finger here, see my hands, reach out and put it in my side." And Thomas knew it was truly Jesus as he touched the scars he wished he could heal, so undeserving was his Lord to have ever received them. Joy washed over him as he cried out, "My Lord and my God!" As easily as Jesus had entered the room though the doors were locked, He now transcended the walls that Thomas had built to insulate himself from the pain of all that had transpired.

In retrospect Thomas wished that he had been able to believe without seeing, but that simply was not his way. His calculating mind demanded proof. It was proof that always led him to a sound decision. He had no problem following once he knew what was going on, but he was not of the persuasion to follow after nebulous pursuits. But now none of this mattered. Jesus was alive. He was in their midst. This was monumental to Thomas in a deeper way than he could explain. Many had come and gone in his life, making promises they never kept. But Jesus had kept His promises. Jesus had proven Himself to him. He had earned his trust. From this point on, Thomas could receive whatever He said without question, demanding no proof. Based on the consistent nature of Jesus, He knew His Word was true. And that was enough regardless of what his eyes saw. This was liberating. He was free to believe, no longer bound by the natural. He was finally able to embrace a deeper dimension of living. Yes, Jesus would leave them again in body, but His Spirit would remain with them. Though invisible, this was fact, and as adamantly as Thomas once doubted, he now believed.

Do you ever struggle to believe that there is a dimension beyond what our natural eye can see where life continues? There is a Word that is true, though we have no physical evidence of it. We must yield to the confirmation of our spirits to confirm what has been revealed. Jesus came, Jesus died, Jesus rose—these are all facts that none of us were physically present to witness. Yet our inner man exuberantly rejoices, "It is true indeed." Though we do not see Him, we know that He is present in the heavenlies, interceding on our behalf in the midst of directing our paths and encouraging us to continue onward. Even as we do not see the wind, we feel it. And so we feel Jesus in every silent moment where tears flow, in every victory small or large, in the miracles of life, from birth to healing to smiling in spite of our pain. He is ever present, the invisible thread that holds the entire fabric of our lives together. This we cannot point to with our finger in any specific place but our hearts. We just simply *know*.

*Dear Heavenly Father, truly we walk by faith and
not by sight. Keep me ever aware of Your presence. In
the times when I cannot sense Your nearness cause
me to rely on the constancy of Your Word. Because
You are my Father and my Friend, I know that You
can be trusted to do as You say. I hold Your promises
dear to my heart. My expectancy is of You. When I
stumble in doubt, help my unbelief and renew my
faith in You. Help my love for You to overshadow the
disappointments I have experienced with others and
never let me see You in the same light, for You tran-
scend our earthly understanding of love and trust.
Heal, build, and restore the wounded places in my
heart that cause me to question You. Meet me in the
place where I reach to see You more clearly, and help
me to rest in Your Word. In Jesus' name, amen.*

Despairing Times

They asked her, "Woman why are you crying?"
"They have taken my Lord away," she said,
"and I don't know where they have put him."

JOHN 20:13

espair washed over Mary like waves upon the ocean. Huge waves, billows pounding against her soul. She had come seeking a little comfort. As much comfort as she could receive at the grave of her Lord, and now she found this—the stone had been rolled away! Well, it must have rolled onto her heart for she felt as if it were breaking beneath the weight of this new occurrence. When would it end? All of the events of the past few days played over and over in her mind. They had taken her Lord. They had beaten Him, bruised Him, and led Him away to be crucified. Mary wished she could have died with Him, so great was her agony. The aloneness that washed over her as His life ebbed away could not be described. She felt as if her heart was breaking, yet she was forced to continue on. For what, she knew not. And so she had merely existed on barely more than soothing memories for these past few days. How would she get through a day without Him? He was the reason she was alive today. He had redeemed her life when no one thought her worthy of the least consideration. And though she was no longer alone, she felt alone deep within the intimate passages of her heart where no man could venture except for Jesus. Jesus was the only One who had touched her there, and now He was gone.

On this morning she hoped to go and anoint Him with spices and just languish in His presence for a little while, perhaps finding a morsel of hope to spur her onward. Though He was dead, just the nearness of His remembrance would suffice to strengthen her resolve to hold on. But now even this small spark of hope had been snatched cruelly from her. He was gone. Gone! The words echoed through every cell of Mary's being. His absence stripped her even further, leaving her feeling completely defenseless and vulnerable. Her sobs filled the garden as all the pain in her heart poured out of her inner being. And then she saw them. Or were they simply a vision seen through the veil of her tears? Two men dressed in white looking like angels! "Woman, why are you crying?" they asked. *Why was she crying?* Wasn't it obvious? The One most dear to her had been taken away. Not once but twice, and it was more than she could bear. And then another stood behind her. "Who are you looking for?" He questioned. She wanted no more questions, only answers. Where had they taken Him? Mary would have no peace until she saw Him again.

And then He called her name. "Mary!" It was like music. An old familiar song that warmed her just so. "Mary!" So melodic. So filled with compassion. Only One had called her name in such a manner. Her heart leapt back to life, following her outward movement as she rushed toward

Jesus to embrace Him. But He cautioned her against touching Him in His present state. For He had not yet ascended to His Father, holy and untouched. Now that she had seen Him, she was released to go and tell the others that He was alive and well. He was alive! Yes, alive! He had not left her like all the others she had known. Though He would be gone physically, He would always be alive and with her in Spirit. She was not alone anymore. With this knowledge Mary's heart took wing as she hastened to tell the others.

To find One who is a haven for our
emotions is a rare and precious gift.

Do you ever feel that you cannot find a real refuge? It is so difficult to find a secure place to rest our fears, our hearts, our weary spirits. The world tears pieces out of our self-worth and soundness of heart each and every day. To find One who is a haven for our emotions is a rare and precious gift. To have this sort of friendship interrupted or severed abruptly can be a jolt to the system that causes us to question if any hope is left. Just as we become adjusted and used to our surroundings, the rug is snatched out from beneath our feet. We feel forsaken, hung out to dry on the line of life. But Jesus comes just as we feel the threat of drowning in our tears, reminding us that He will never leave us or forsake us. That He is just a prayer away.

Still attentive to our every cry. Still a Comforter we can rely on when all others fail.

Dear Heavenly Father, I have struggled in this place before—this place of immense disappointment and loss. I need You to touch me. Revive me. Affirm me. As I reach out to You, let me feel You in a whole new way. A way that makes You more real than You've ever been to me before. My heart cries to find You. My spirit longs to embrace You and draw You near. Make Yourself known to me. Let me find You in the midst of all that strives to keep us separate. Silence the voice of the enemy that whispers doubts of Your love for me. Let my trust in Your constant presence be established. Truly, You will never leave me or forsake me. Holy Spirit, speak to me, breathe words of refreshment over me, and let the Word of God come alive in me, filling me with the type of joy that the world cannot take away. In Jesus' name, amen.

And at the ninth hour
Jesus cried with a loud voice, saying,
Eloi, Eloi, lama sabachthani?
which is, being interpreted,
My God, my God,
why hast thou forsaken me?

MARK 15:34 KJV

Prayerful Times

*He took Peter and the two sons of Zebedee along with him,
and he began to be sorrowful and troubled. Then he said
to them, "My soul is overwhelmed with sorrow to
the point of death. Stay here and keep watch with me."*

MATTHEW 26:38

They couldn't stay awake and pray for Him
even for just one hour. One little hour! How long had He
been with them? Three years? Sometimes it felt like ninety,
and yet it would now be over too soon. He loved His disciples. They were made up of the most interesting con-
glomeration of personalities and temperaments. There was
Peter, who always had to have the last word in any given
conversation. John, who loved Him. James, with his thun-
derous temper. He loved them all. They were good men—
all twelve—sincere even when they were wrong. They
gave their all; they put their faith in Him. At times that
faith was a bit misplaced, but nevertheless they were
steadfast. Needless to say, they had kept life interesting.

He gazed at them as they slept now, completely out of
tune with what was about to occur. He thought of the

others—Matthew, Mark, Philip...on and on His mind scanned through images of them in His head as if looking at them for the last time. He stopped at Judas. Poor Judas—he had opened himself up to be used as an instrument of the devil. How this deceived one would suffer after He was gone! Judas would never know that all was well, that Jesus had to die to save them all. He thought of the upcoming days and His eyes grew dark with pain. Pain for the agony He knew they would experience because of their continued lack of understanding. They would see soon enough. And then a greater pain washed over Him.

Though He had volunteered for the mission of giving His life so that the world through Him might be saved, the process would be a difficult one, like nothing He had ever before experienced. He literally would take on the sins of the world. He who knew no sin would become sin. But in the process He would be separated from the Father. He had never been separated from Him, and the thought of it was unbearable. It brought a violent shock to His system, so extreme that He sweated drops of blood as He prayed one last prayer for the disciples. For the world. For Himself. From the beginning it had been Him, His Father, and the Holy Ghost, so close that they were one. Extensions of each other. Literally beginning and ending one another's sentences. All that He was and all that He did revolved around the Father. He lived for Him. He breathed for Him. He had his very being in Him. Conversing with Him was like breathing. He couldn't bear the thought of having their fellowship broken. To not experience divine intimacy with Him was worse than anything He could imagine. He would rather experience anything but that. No matter how brief the time of their separation, it would seem an eternity. He would die a million deaths inside, though His body would only go through one.

But He was determined to complete what He had started. He only wished that there was another way. And then His attentions turned to the disciples and all of those He had taught. He prayed that the Father would keep them. They, too, would go through the bitterness of separation and much heartache. In this He had the advantage. He knew what was happening; they did not. They had yet to truly perceive the meaning of all that He had told them. Their confusion would be great, and He prayed that they would not scatter. But He also knew that the suffering they were about to encounter would produce perseverance and character. In light of this they would be strengthened to have immovable hope. Oh, He could see what these men would become once they endured this test. Fearless, mighty men of God. It made His present pain worthwhile.

He longed for the day when He would show them around heaven and they would see His glory. It was so far beyond their comprehension that He had not even tried to describe it to them. They only knew Him as He was with them on earth; they did not know another side of Him— the side where He sat among the host of heaven, exalted above every name. His garments gleamed and the holiness of God shone forth from Him like gold. The side where He was one with the Father. He wanted them to see and experience this, to have that same oneness. To be free from all that bound them on earth. This was His prayer and the expectancy that spurred Him toward the finish line. As He looked beyond the disciples down through the pages of time, He saw the names of the others who were written in the Lamb's Book of Life. All of those people He already knew would come to be a part of the Bride of Christ, joined forever with Him in eternity—you and I joyfully being among that number—and He also prayed for us! That we would be partakers of all that He was and have fellowship with the Father unbroken throughout eternity.

And then He rose to the occasion and went forth to meet His fate, strong in His resolve to have us all by His side forever. He was accused, abused, beaten, and crucified. As He became sin for us, God turned His face from Him, unable to bear the stench of sin in His nostrils. And then the moment Jesus most dreaded came to pass. His soul was ripped, His spirit shattered by the vast void of darkness as He felt the light of God removed from Him. How great a darkness it was! While others wondered at how quickly He died, commenting on how unusual it was, they failed to recognize that no cross could kill Him. Only separation from His Father could. He gave up His life rather than endure the torture of this state. But then on the third day He rose and ascended back to the Father. In parting from the disciples this one last time, He sympathized with their pain caused by the separation and promised them a Comforter, a deposit of Himself that would be with them until they met again. They must trust and know that they would never be alone.

How important is your relationship with God to you? We have all offended a loved one and felt the pain of separation. But how many of us despair over being separated from our Heavenly Father? As we move from fear to faith to love in our Christian experience, we are subject to different depths of emotions toward God. Most of us have an intellectual understanding of who God is and what Christ did for us, and we are quite content to keep our relationship with Them at face value. We are grateful, acknowledging that we need what they have to offer, and we're content to leave it at that. But there is another place where a deeper and sweeter coexistence can take place. When we truly fall in love with Jesus, embrace our Abba Father, and walk in total dependence on the leading of the Holy Spirit, something happens. A powerful connection. A love connection. The fellowship and intimacy that comes out of that is addictive. So sweet, so rich, so all-consumingly satisfying, we will crave it always. And though many things assault us each and every day that threaten to separate us from our love source, the thought of separation becomes overwhelming. We find ourselves scurrying back to our rightful position, resuming the flow of intimacy. Reveling in His love for us. Never alone.

Dear Heavenly Father, thank You for all You have done for me. Thank You for loving me enough to give Yourself totally through Your Son Jesus to redeem me. Thank You for the interest You show in every little detail of my life, for sending me a Comforter to lead and guide me. But most of all I am overwhelmed by Your constant and faithful love. I simply ask You this: Fill me to overflowing with love for You. Let it seep out of every part of me and let everything I do be an outpouring of my adoration for You. I am not seeking a religious experience; I crave true relationship with You. I ask You to teach me the things that Jesus knew. Show me the secrets of how to have the same type of relationship that He had with You. I want to be a true son (or daughter), able to rest in the knowledge that You and I are One. Forever One. In Jesus' name, amen.

If you would like to correspond with Michelle
in response to her books, contact her at:

Michelle McKinney Hammond
c/o Heartwing Ministries
PO Box 11052
Chicago, IL 60611-1722

E-mail: heartwingmin@yahoo.com
Website: http://www.heartwing.com

For speaking engagements, contact:

Speak Up Speaker Services
1-800-870-7719